RESIDENT
TOURIST
Los Angeles

RESIDENT TOURIST

TOURIST

Los Angeles

Kelly Mayfield,

Chuck Mindenhall, and

Aaron M. Fontana

LA
WEEKLY
BOOKS

An LA Weekly Book for St. Martin's Press / New York

LA Weekly books is a trademark of LA Weekly Media, Inc.

www.stmartins.com

Design by Phil Mazzone

ISBN 0-312-29060-8

First Edition: December 2002

10 9 8 7 6 5 4 3 2 1

Contents

CONTENTS

CONTENTS

Acknowledgments

Kelly would like to thank Judy Jablonski Proffer for her faith and imagination and her family for everything. Kindest regards.

Chuck would like to thank Red for her help with the organization and compilation of this book's listings, Nina Hartley, Lord Christ, Stan Bolinowitz, T. R. Dunn for inspiration, Mom, Angel, Robert, Tommy Apodaca, "the stick" Jakib Abdul J'Marlen, the White Shadow, Sir Rider Haggard, Rio Claro beer for ranting (ranting, like ranting, you know?), Lisa Lincoln for the photos that never made the book, Kimo, Bruce Hazel and Billy Staff, Michael Connor and Elizabeth, my precious coauthors, and finally, Judy Jablonski Proffer for inventing this most abusive assignment.

Aaron would like to thank his family for their support; Jade Chang, for her astounding patience, advice, friendship, and love; Judy for everything; Michael Connor at St. Martin's Press; Chuck Mindenhall for involving me in the first place; and the city of Los Angeles.

Preface

Welcome, Resident Tourist!

When you come to Los Angeles, you're bombarded with lots of big, famous things to see. Go see some of it. It is your destiny to visit Universal Studios and see "The Parting of the Red Sea" and the *Jaws* set on the Backlot Tram Tour. Don't be afraid! Go to Disneyland! See some sites! When you are ready to have L.A. shown to you by an old friend who's a local, call us. Our goal is to have you experience this city from the perspective of a street-crawling, seriously observant, kind-of-wacky pal who absolutely *needs* to show you all his or her special places, be they well known or not. They'll drag you to some obscure corner of Los Angeles, and behold, it's a gem.

You'll find restaurants, watering holes, shopping, sites, all sorts of odds and sods. It's a journey, and if you're lucky enough to live here, one you can take over time. It's not an attempt to be comprehensive; if something's in here, it's because one of the authors likes it a lot.

And now it's time for a shameless plug that happens to be a truth so I reserve the right to *not* feel guilty. When you first arrive, grab a copy of *LA Weekly*. You can pick it up all over town, but check record stores and interesting boutiques first. In the interest of full disclosure, all three authors have worked or are working at the *Weekly*, but regardless, it's still the best deal in town. The calendar section will give you a blow-by-blow for each day of the week and will provide you with the most current information for nightlife. Especially if your aim is live music, this will provide you a complete itinerary, and it's free!

A word of caution: Please call to confirm hours and any specific information. We don't want you to get stuck because something doesn't have normal hours.

So be you tourist or be you resident, may you discover something new today.

—Kelly Mayfield,
coauthor of this illuminating, though less filling, book

Welcome to Los Angeles, California, consumer. A fine city it is, if you know where to go and what to do. But chances are you don't, whether you're a tourist from Singapore or a resident of thirty years. So we here at *Resident Tourist*, a collection of three separate writers with very different perspectives on the city, have taken this opportunity to put on our navigational hats and become your pocket tour guide—which beats the hell out of a regular in-the-flesh friend, who gets tired of showing you around after a couple of days.

So much of what exists right under our noses we pass by without even noticing on our way to a taping of *The Price Is Right*, or heading to the beach or Magic Mountain. Who saw that

Russian deli on Santa Monica Boulevard, and who knew they had
the best pastry in town? Who saw the salon with the girls in cutoff shorts on Ventura Boulevard, who wiggle so neatly for "present extras"? Not you people, that's for sure. You were pushing the
speed limit to get to the Wax Museum before hitting Universal
Studios. That is inherently wrong, and that is why we are here: to
show you, the resident, the tourist, the do-gooder, the theologian,
the acrobat, the fishmonger, the loving father of three beautiful
daughters, the someday ancestor, the uncle in the van who the
family doesn't talk about anymore, et alia, to show *you* . . . where
to go. Selfless, we know.

Welcome to *our* Los Angeles, this sprawling immensity that we
have narrowed into the thin crisp pages that lay before you. It is
with tremendous affection that we, your triumvirate of qualified
Los Angeles "off-the-beaten-trail" experts, provide a refreshing
guide for getting around, like that dear hip friend who simply
doesn't exist. We are unapologetic at *Resident Tourist*, because we
don't like suckers who drop money on worn-out, boring sights.
We least of all like convention and common expectation. To hell
with single-file cattle lines. And we hate the vogue. We like
thinkers, people who have culture and an eye out for adventure—
we like *you*!

Beware of internal ennui, reader: Los Angeles has ways of
reducing you into an awestruck Viper Room frequenter. Or worse
yet, a roaming vagabond with handheld camera filming the spittle
on Hollywood Boulevard. We see it every day, and we long to
right the ship. The Los Angeles that unfolds before you through
our eyes is one of cumulative years of research, insight, and experience. We cover aspects of Los Angeles that are less in the spotlight, lighter on the pocketbook, sincerer in their business
practices, longer in the tooth, and truer in their aims. From Ma
and Pa businesses to places to hike and exercise, to truly unique
places to get something to eat, we have uncovered it.

This guide is not entirely comprehensive. It is a "taste" book, put together randomly by our writers to take you in hand to the places that *we* enjoy. We write without prejudice, and we search out greater meanings in the popular places to go. In short, we are putting forth uniqueness rather than bothering you with the commonplace. So, when you go home to Baton Rouge (or wherever the hell you came from), our goal is for you to tell your envious friends, "I ate at Roscoe's Chicken and Waffles on Gower, and I'll be damned if Snoopy Dog-Dog wasn't sitting next to me!" Some bullshit like that. Something different. Something new. Something that makes you feel like you really visited Los Angeles, instead of walking like a somnambulist through our jaded streets. And if you live right here in Los Angeles, we say, "You're welcome, don't mention it. It was our pleasure, no problem." And next time you cross paths with some incurable mainstreamer, hike a leg to him and pee.

—Chuck Mindenhall,
coauthor of this semirandom, incomprehensive book

People who haven't lived in L.A. always give me that line about how it's a plastic city with fake people. Come to think of it, people I know that live here sometimes give me that, too. I always tell them the same thing, that that really hasn't been my experience here at all; but then, I don't often hang out with people who are apt to spend their Friday night trying to convince a door bouncer to let them in their exclusive club; nor have I ever (sure, I *considered* once or twice) experienced the cattle-call procedure of, say, a soap-opera audition.

My point is that, in my experience, L.A. is what you make it to be; and for that matter, L.A. is what you make yourself to be. Sure, if you're a gambling sort, you might opt to come here instead of Vegas to strike it big in the acting biz; and you might get jaded, too. If you're an ingénue, you might simply get hurt. And if you're expecting great things from the city, you might get disappointed. But then, maybe you didn't expect enough of yourself.

As for me, my L.A. is a place where I came, some years back, as an immature young man and grew to be one who was (albeit still immature in other ways), better somehow; L.A. is a place where I began to realize my hopes of becoming a writer; L.A. is the place where I have met a lot of interesting people, and, sure, lost some (or even left them behind), too, along the way; L.A. is also the place where I found people that I'll always have in my life; and it's a place where I usually feel comfortable.

In short, L.A. is, for good and bad, now my home.

And as everybody has a different vision of what home is, I, too, have mine. The following will give you an idea of how I see Los Angeles. But if you don't read any further, I can tell you right now that the city to me is a wonderful, but occasionally crappy, place with many awesome things to do and see; and it's a place that I love.

I'd like to dedicate this book to my family in Michigan, who don't think of L.A. as a fake place at all; and to Jade, who does live here and says good things about it.

—Aaron M. Fontana,

coauthor of this pessimistic yet hopeful and sprightly Los Angeles account

RESIDENT TOURIST

Los Angeles

CHAPTER 1

Adult Los Angeles

Breaking In to Adult Video

Fisting is legal in Los Angeles—praise the lord! But fisting is *illegal* on film. There are currently a few debates going on in our court system as to what constitutes a "fist," which befogs the whole subject in the first place, thus making it difficult to nail down your technique with a clear conscious. An artistic quandary, perhaps? I personally am no expert on the matter. I only know this much because Nina Hartley, the internationally acclaimed pornstress of over 570 adult films, told me so. Actually, she told a whole group of shady middle-aged oddballs who attended her seminar at the Learning Annex in Santa Monica the same thing. Twenty-one men and one brave woman—undoubtedly a nymphomaniac much the same as the self-professed Nina—sat through a three-hour discourse on how to make the pornographic film and video industry a career. It was as strange as

1

a covert cabal meeting to discuss alternative theologies or how to uproot boring Samaritan life. Only, we were talking about doggy-style grinding, money shots, and naked, willing girls. Talk about an evening well spent! I only wish I had brought along a flask of something strong for my nerves, and a camera to prove the existence of Neanderthal man.

Nina-bleeping-Hartley (!), folks, the very same who starred in *The Ultimate Lover*, an admitted sex fiend and known polygamist, whose exhibitionism and overglowing libertinism are as transparent as Caribbean seawater. She was admirably candid and to the point—unapologetic, an absolute realist. And that body! Oh, that body of hers has a story or two to tell.

What I wanted to know was where the dotted line for me to sign was. All she did, though, was shatter my vision of becoming the next Smoky Evans (which is my pet/street-porn name, if I may add a certain cliché to this mix). From the get-go the adult industry, which I had heretofore held up on the highest pedestal, took on the grimmest image. Grisly stories were told, of corruption and greed, of artistic integrity and lack thereof, of bitchy females and cold hot tubs, of casting calls and arrests and legations and disease tests and cocaine and—heaven forbid—uncooperative penises! Good gravy, I'd thought it was all about scoring assorted chicks without the trial-and-error process!

But I was wrong. Nina told me so. And she discouraged us all from getting too giddy about the prospect of successfully breaking in to adult video. She started with: "How many of you want to work on camera?" None of us raised our hands, though many of us wanted, indeed, to be on film. "None of you? Well, then, you will not make a dime in the adult video industry." She really told us! All of the future "directors" and "producers" and "writers" in the room were bound for penury. You could feel the spirit of the room drop, sag, wane, and then depart altogether. (It returned later during the question/answer round.) And that started a three-hour pornographic denunciation on why the adult industry is solely for hobbyists and freaks—not for enterprise, commerce, spiritual gain, or amiable recognition (though there are case examples of each of these where people have been successful). This forty-year-old fox, with a rump that rotates on an axis and a lisp that made sex sound so filthy ("*sthex*"), was deflating the room as quickly as she was exciting it with her English-style horse-riding britches. Let me review my notes. Ah, yes, and in the process, let me dampen your hopes of being a member of the porn community.

Did you know that ten thousand pornographic videos are released every year? (With an average of five sex scenes per feature, that's fifty thousand scenes of anal, oral, traditional, gay, straight, and bisexual acts and any other kind of exhibitionism caught on tape for consumer masturbatory pleasure.) Neither did I. There is nothing out there that hasn't been done, no fetish uncovered, nothing so unthinkably degrading the French didn't concoct many moons ago. Almost exclusively, these films are shot in the San Fernando Valley, right here in our diverse little town. Lucky for those of us who appreciate the liberal arts! Pornography was legalized in 1972 in certain areas of California (Sacramento and the Bay area, in particular), and finally in 1988 in Los Angeles (four years into Ms. Hartley's career), and hardcore pornography remains illegal in certain states. The average budget for a feature porn film is $10,000, with the highest of the year 2000 being a whopping $150,000—or the equivalent of food-catering costs to a big-budget Hollywood movie like *Planet of the Apes*. The adult industry is still fairly primitive/intimate in how they conduct business, with agreements being reached on a handshake, and with the inner circle of the existing porn family holding all the cards, while the ebb and tide (and ebb) of newcomers trying to get in are treated like set towels (and we know how set towels are treated!). With the guerrilla ways in which they act, direct, and produce, one cannot carry shame into porn. One must

RESIDENT TOURIST: LOS ANGELES

come in 100 percent committed to this lifestyle, and have a sense of irony. Otherwise, we are told, things get ugly.

There is a lot of paperwork involved in making a pornographic movie, such as permits—$550 a week, in most cases, plus location fees—and model releases (mandatory), as well as HIV testing papers (which need to be updated every other month) and pre-production rentals (video, props, etc.). A typical half-day of shooting lasts eight hours, and a full day, twelve. Most actresses/ actors appear in two sex scenes per feature. Men stars average between $300 and $500 a sex scene, while women get anywhere from $500 to $800. These numbers are based on *what* they are performing, and what kind of name they have, though seniority means nothing in this business, and the scale plateaus at $1,000 for the biggest stars. Many porn stars do two to three features *a week*. Like numbers? How about this stat: As a porn star, your ratio of being accepted among family, friends, loved ones, and supporters, compared to those opposed, will teeter toward those opposed— *way* toward the opposition. You will become a black sheep and a pariah, and there is no turning back once the film is out there. The attention you will receive is by far more negative than positive, and the money isn't so great as to make that sacrifice. Thinking it will be a step toward a larger career is wrong, too. Very few people transition into Hollywood pictures after being porn stars, because they are considered plague. And yes, that includes Traci Lords (we remember *Melrose Place*). Bear in mind, Nina Hartley was a costar in Paul Anderson's *Boogie Nights*—and what was her role? An ultraslut! The segues into greater fame are nonexistent.

You're a man, and you're still not deterred from making it in adult film. That's understandable. I needed more discouragement, too. Casting calls are at nine A.M., normally. As a man, you must show up on time, get "excited" next to a crew of cameramen and male directors (there are *no* "fluffers," as the rumor has it), and then maintain this arousal for hours while still shots are taken (for the box label and magazines), and then perform on cue from

every angle, with a hot camera on your exposed goods, and the
twenty male onlookers. Average sex scenes are twelve minutes
long in the finished product, but the average shooting time is
ninety minutes to two hours, which is an awful lot of "sustain-
ing"! In the exact words of Nina: "There is nothing more humil-
iating than when an amateur male struggles with his erection. It is
the most embarrassing thing to see happen." Sure, there is Viagra
and penile injections, but consider the inhuman pace. Take into
account that the female may be cold, callous, businesslike, passion-
less, shallow . . . And you may be wearing a condom, depending
on the director (some are traditional and stubborn, others safer). It
takes a special kind of male to be a pro in this industry, usually a
degenerate of some kind with no home life. My kind of guy, but
rare all the same. "For the man, it is 95 percent mental, and 5 percent physical," stated Nina, whom you tend to believe when you
stop to think that she has been at this for seventeen years! That is
a hard distinction to make when you are dumb enough to get
yourself involved in this mess in the first place. Still not dissuaded?
You need plenty of inches, too, smart-guy.

We learned about more than a flat list of interesting statistics,
averages, percentages, and numbers, though. The concept that
pornography is better as a spectator sport, from the sidelines rather
than being in the game, was pounded home. We learned that
video killed the Pussycat Theater, and that sound quality in film is
held in the lowest regards. (With the exception of Blake Anderson's films, which Nina adores, saying this: "The actors are paint;
Blake is the artist.") You all know how poor the overdubbed
soundtracks are! We also learned that a forty-year-old woman can
sprawl out on a table before twenty-one very questionable men
and one lone woman, and reenact a sex scene without feeling vio-
lated or threatened, and then yawn with practiced indifference
moments later and check her cell-phone clock without acknowl-
edging the simmering whistle of our blood rising. But mostly we
learned that porn movies are for independently wealthy people

who want a hobby; or orphans, lost souls, sex fiends, attention-starved people, broken people, or, sadly enough, teenage girls who are willing to do anything to make a dollar. The somberness of the industry was not sugarcoated in any way, nor represented with any kind of optimism from Ms. Hartley. It was put forth in the crass way that it exists. The point of the class was to weed out the disillusioned, and to prepare our testosterone pressure-valves for alternative outlets. How eloquent she was, that Nina, lisp and all, and how brutally honest.

Nevertheless, a trip to the **World Modeling Agency** in Sherman Oaks, the porn capital of the world, all bottled under one roof, may resurrect these disillusions. They have a way of recruiting youthful willingness like an awestruck practitioner of black magic. I know—I used to wait tables right next door at the glorified McDonald's (aka Hamburger Hamlet), where I served the head honcho and an ever-changing pack of freshly conscribed new faces, Lee Press-on Nails, and silicone implants. Jim, here's to your generous gratuities! You dirty birdie . . .

Here, Kitty, Kitty, Kitty

So there's this little theater down on Sunset and Western that shows skin flicks, right? Sure does. It has all the shade of a red-wood forest, and the April-freshness of, uh, some recently cleaned linens, let's say. Now, usually pornographic films are reserved for bedrooms and key parties, but at this quasi-landmark, the appeal is in the prospect of seeing the "money shot" on the big screen (check local listings for 3-D matinees). We all know that video and DVD have all but killed the art of big-screen porn—sad but true. Nevertheless, go check out Pussycat Theater and marvel at the intimacies of a couple or three lovers engaged in licentious behavior in a public forum. Don't mind the activities of your neighbor, or that strange asthmatic man behind you, they are part of the allure; they are décor. Come on: Don't let another great film like *The Banalities of Analities* pass through the theaters straight to VHS without a viewing at the movie house! I know that I sure regretted missing *Deep into Martha's Cave* when it was out two years ago. Must be eighteen years old to enter (nudge, nudge). Public indecency is not recommended (wink, wink). Movies rotate with frequency, so don't hesitate when the film you want to see comes out. Ticket prices are $8 ($5 for seniors). Open 11 A.M.–3 A.M. daily.

Pussycat Theater
1508 Western Avenue, Los Angeles

The Juxtaposition of Adjectives

Always walking the fine line between two unlikely adjectives (those being "sexy" and "scary"), this L.A. institution of a strip club and bar is tattered but always has something to see onstage. The last time I was there, one dancer, who looked like she might be a man, put a lit cigarette between her legs as if she was trying to get the nether body part down there to smoke it. The crowd— made up of drunken regulars and slumming Hollywood star and starlet types (yes, girls come, too; it's part of the fun)—didn't know whether to cry, laugh, or run. So they just doled out the dollar bills, throwing them madly onstage. The stripper, pleased of course, tried to arch her back to make her body into an upside-down U, but kept losing her balance and had to straighten back up to try, again and again. It was not exactly . . . alluring. But then again, it kind of was. Yes, what they lack in coordination here, they make up for in heaps of, um, eclectic panache. And unlike most of the other L.A. strip clubs, where you walk in and are almost immediately deprived of $60 by drink minimums and tip-mad ladies (who have the protection of mean-looking bouncers), Jumbo's approach is much more billfold-friendly.

Jumbo's Clown Room
5153 Hollywood Boulevard, Hollywood
(323) 666-1187

A Reason to Be Optimistic About the World

Casey, the bartender, is a full-blooded blond Italian with an Irish clover tattooed on her shoulder. "This is basically a local bar, with regulars, kind of like *Cheers*." So it is, Casey, so it is. But the twenty-five-year-old establishment holds a certain subterranean lure, like it was intended to be a neighborhood watering hole yet became a drunken catering-house to semiserious writers, fishermen, attorneys, and "young, dumb, and full of cum"s, all lifting their beers in unison. What's it like? you ask. The restrooms are located conveniently up front, near the doorman; soaps in there are cherry-almond. The jukebox, always with a woman making selections on it, plays a lot of glam-era favorites, mixed with the occasional Neil Diamond. Offensive neon beer signs of all sorts make the small room increasingly, and sublimely, bright. The smoke forms dollar signs and music notes in these lights, and the pupils never dilate. Three pool tables are obtrusively placed around the perimeter of the . . . stages. Oh yeah . . . there are strippers on those stages. Long-legged and in full violet blossom, working a four- to five-girl rotation to the stale wits with the $7.25 pitchers of domestic. One of the girls mechanically surveys her viewing audience while on her back, through scissoring legs. Another, on the "main stage," does a perfunctory strut before a rather subdued threesome seated barside. No cover charge. Ah, life . . . how you spoil us! Open seven days, noon–2 A.M. There is another Candy Cat on Devonshire.

Candy Cat II
6816 Winnetka Avenue, Canoga Park
(818) 999-3187

Good Smut and . . . Coffee?

It's so hard to find a decent sex shop that serves good coffee nowadays. In fact, it seems the only one in this city is Larry Flynt's Hustler Hollywood store, an intriguing combo of café and sexual supply emporium (you got your rubbers, your sexy lingerie, your

8

XXX DVDs) for the discerning dirtball. We love it! Stop in here and grab your double latte, and afterward, walk up and down aisle after filthy aisle of the slickest-looking smut you've ever seen (you'll find no sex booths here). There are sexy coffee-table books and magazines—even newsy stuff for the wimps—for every taste, as well as plenty of stiletto heels and lacy bras for your favorite little sex kitten; the video section is enormous and has everything from your softcore variety to your down-and-dirty *bleep bleep bleep* [CENSORED] penetration flick. Sure, you won't find many people from your church group here; but then we can probably all agree that that's a good thing. And the best thing about it all is that there's free parking in the back. Now, you *really* don't find that a lot here.

Hustler Hollywood
8920 Sunset Boulevard, West Hollywood
(310) 860-9009

Simplicity
So, you're in Los Angeles and the regal Hollywood bar scene hasn't rewarded you yet with a nice piece of tail. It isn't your feathered hair, dude, or your new Chaps cologne—though both are essential chest-smiting signs of bravado and virility, don't feel bad about that. It's just that women have a sick sense when it comes to an aching man's libido, and they know when the pipes of common prowlers are loaded. Don't fret: Go to Santa Monica Boulevard, near Highland Avenue. The most important thing about a good prostitute is the simplistic way in which they have rubbed out the chase. The game is off, gentlemen. The money spent enjoys an immediate result instead of being dished out in monthly installments, where emotions are tangled and misunderstandings take place. There is a decent variety of girls east of Highland Avenue, up Santa Monica (the other direction is a gamble for straight men, and an adventure for adventurous types), operational round-the-clock. You're looking for an amazon woman

with red hair? A mulatto with spiked heels? An orphan with a nose piercing? These streets have them in spades. Fit your fetish with these girls, brothers, and remember that the rules are different on the streets. Prices are not always negotiable, and tips are definitely advisable. And, of course, *Resident Tourist* encourages consumers to sport a raincoat to avoid obvious hazards.

Women for sale
Highland heading east on Santa Monica Boulevard
Cash only

Feline Horny?

One of the less-talked-about strip bars in Los Angeles is Cheetah's in Silver Lake, a rather quirky-looking abnormality from the outside, with beautiful treasures within. Men and women come here, not just to see a dancing girl twirling around a brass pole, but also to have those same girls sit on their laps. The girls at Cheetah's are vaguely natural by Los Angeles standards, which is to say that silicone is not predominant, yet they are ample, and *flexible*. Also predominant is a rather Stanley Kubrick-esque golden-hued bar with purely devilish vixens, clad in leather and vinyl, slinging bottles of Bombay gin and the like. The music is loud, and there is a pool table in the back room. Essentially there aren't any pressures at Cheetah's, because it's a bar first, a strip joint second. Many of the patrons here sit at the bar feeling comfortable watching Clippers basketball on television with the secure knowledge that a leggy nineteen-year-old girl is maneuvering a kind of somersault behind them. Above all, this place is seductively peculiar, with plenty of glass and mirrors and white lights and tightly bound libido bulging in the groin area. Cheetah's is an ideal place to take a son who recently became an adult, or a daughter who is thinking about skipping college.

Cheetah's
4600 Hollywood Boulevard, Silver Lake
(323) 660-6733

CHAPTER 2

Drinking: Bars in Los Angeles

Away from the Pretense: L.A.'s Real Bars

Bars in Hollywood are a commodity for youthful actors, models, writers, film directors, and musicians of every kind; indeed, bars are the scene-defining temples. They are showcases where our city's edgier people come forth and model their newest garb, drink the latest en vogue cocktail, and promote their latest projects. In a real sense, Hollywood bars are dark places. The key words at a typical Hollywood bar are "I am" and "me." Use these enough, and you will fit in nicely as one of the many porcelain figurines who can't pronounce "altruism," much less grasp the meaning. A great many vanity bars, such as Bar Marmont, Sky Bar, and the Sunset Room are heatedly competitive, and thoroughly overpriced, with an ambience is certainly the death of magic. On the whole, the people who go to these bars are struggling to find themselves, and they make people suffer through their tensions. Therefore, in efforts to steer you clear of unfounded spoiledness and corruption, these places have been 86'ed from our listings with your best interests in mind. Remember that greater benevolence exists away from the cast of sleeve-tuggers who can't live without being acknowledged. Real talent is in the *dives*. If "the scene" takes over these bars in the interim between now and when this book goes to print, we apologize. We saw Daddy's die a coward's death when it showed so much promise early on, and The Powerhouse is soon to follow. The following bars are humble and very much a part of Los Angeles' history.

Corridos, Futbol, and Mucho Drinkie

L.A.'s own John Fante would have loved The Landing Strip over by the Van Nuys airport, because it is poetic and the carpet is sticky with beer. It is a Spanish-speaking bar with billiards and Foosball tables, a jukebox with all the Mexican favorites, a small stage, and a capacity of 88 people. Yet lo and behold, the Mexican bands that play there arrive in full-blown, decked-out tour buses fit for Menudo! These magnificent buses sit out in the parking lot sparkling under night lights and stars, next to Volkswagen buses and El Caminos, with an air of supremacy. And the locals say "aw" and "yippee" and make their way into the bar to see what all the hype is about. The place swells with 88 tequila drinkers, and madness meets jollity and glasses clank, and the futbol game or boxing match on television receives grunts and cheers. Cheap beers and shots! And lots of promiscuity! The Landing Strip is as anonymous as it gets, because people are drunk. And hey, what a great place to *be* drunk! The Landing Strip is a staple of Van Nuys, which *Resident Tourist* happens to admire very much.

The Landing Strip
16453 Vanowen Boulevard, Van Nuys
Phone number not listed in the book. Just go, you'll dig.

Topanga: It's Australian for Occultism, Mate!

Tucked away in the Topanga Canyon jungle, near the trickle of a small stream, is a place called Wendy's California Trail, where Australians and Americans alike go for pints of "bee-ah," billiards, sports-watching, and roughnecking. The reason we like it is that those Aussies are so damn sweet, the pints are cheap, and the foundations of vanity are nonexistent. And that's not all—we are also thankful for the manmade fountain that reminds one that he has to pee all the time. Wendy's serves up delightful food, too, like pizza and sandwiches and whatnot, and has an outdoor patio to digest these vittles during magnificent crepuscule. Plus they talk all Australian, you know. With accents and everything! There are Australian flags and Australian maps on the walls and even Australian *piquancy*, which, we were told, means something nice. There is even a guitarist who plays awesomely, sometimes while donnybrooks are taking place, other times when mud-wrestling is on the bar television.

Wendy's California Trail
1704 N. Topanga Canyon Boulevard, Topanga
(310) 455-7111

A Time for Shuffleboard

The Barrel in Sherman Oaks is a "let it all hang out" bar, perfect to hit after a grueling day of hard work and slow capitulation to the dollar sign. The crowd here is mixed, with old and young alike, giving both generations a chance to mince words and arm-wrestle over a mug of cold ale. But remember, the idea here is intoxication. Inexpensive drinks at The Barrel give it a certain allure, but it is the shuffleboard table that ultimately grabbed our attention here at *Resident Tourist*. The smooth oaken surface of the board top, lightly sprinkled with fine grains of sand, gives those pucks the illusion of floating in space. Go ahead, get drunk like I did and play a game against Neil Patrick Harris (aka Doogie Howser, M.D.) and show him who the true precocious one is! Brainchild, my ass—I beat him in straight sets! There is also a pool table to get your billiards on with, and televisions showing various sporting events. And that good ol' jukebox in the back will give you all the background theme music you need when you win a couple of games of shuffleboard and imagine yourself in slow motion on ESPN. The place is full of live-action highlight reels. Now, if they could only solve the plumbing problems.

The Barrel
4547 Van Nuys Boulevard, Sherman Oaks
(818) 501-9202

Phew! That Was Close!

A bad scenario, Romeo! You went out last night with your mistress and the home front has grown suspect of your whereabouts. She demands an explanation—and pronto. Uh-oh! What to do? All right, obviously you are an iniquitous fellow, and you must learn a thing or two about cover-up schemes, but for the love of mankind, have your cake and eat it, too. You will get yours in the end, but not right now. Not on *Resident Tourist*'s watch. Tell her you were at The Alibi Room in Culver City. For crud's sake, that's why it's there! They will provide you some shade when the interrogations get hot. "Sure enough"—they will answer her inquiries—"he was seated at the end barstool for hours." Meanwhile you and your mistress can live to see another night. Plus The Alibi Room is full of regulars you can get to know on a first-name basis. People speak a certain language here, a kind of argot, a cross between boat-speak and pig Latin. This also will help obscure things to your benefit. Slurring, swaying, singing sweet little "alibis"—these are the lyrics of love. And Donovan's "Hurdy Gurdy Man" is on the juker. Paradise! Opens at 6 A.M. daily. Need I laud it any more?

The Alibi Room
12236 Washington Boulevard, Culver City
(310) 398-5516

Koreatown and Winos

Temperatures are soaring into the mid-80s, and the palate is parched. You are somewhere between downtown and Hollywood, and feeling a little culture-shocked because all the writing around you is Korean. Duck into Frank and Hank's cocktail lounge for spiritual guidance and a sense of absolution. They have "the coldest beer in town"! That's right, they store their beer in refrigerators a few degrees lower than other bars. It will beat the smoke out of the brain; that's a gimme. This is a bottom-of-the-line Bukowskian bar, where people smoke cigarettes, shoot darts and pool, argue, curse, ramble, fumble, and play electronic card games. But they mostly drink. And there is always elbow room because the pretty boys and girls of Hollywood, who always attempt to make all the run-down watering holes throughout the vicinity upscale, are no match for the regular clientele here. Forget about the vogue. You order a cosmopolitan here, and you're likely to be spat on! (That last part was dreamed up for effect.) Beer, whiskey, bourbon, hair of the dog, tequila—these are the drinks at Frank and Hank's. Leave the schoolgirl stuff to the trend-guzzlers. This place requires a little hair on the chest (or at least a tattoo on the chest, for proper ladies).

Frank and Hank's
518 S. Western Avenue, Koreatown
(213) 383-2087

The White Horse: Don't Ride the White Pony

"The White Horse is a dive bar," a friend once told me. Should have sucker-punched him right then and there, and replied, "Dear sir, you have no *soul!*" Indeed, the location is questionable, being only a couple of doors from the famed **Pussycat Theater** (see chapter 1) on Western, but the entrails are flush with red regality and opulence. Everything is spick-and-span, Daddy-o. Dive bar? Not really—not *yet* anyway. It has been around since 1985, and plays host to a great many private parties (book your bachelor party there, or a birthday). Play free pool Sunday through Wednesday of each week; and owner Victoria Lelea loves to feed her soused late-night crowd hot dogs and microwave popcorn. "Not exactly dive material," I would like to say to my brotherless friend. Hell, the stuffed animals and potpourri that are awkwardly placed throughout the bar took me aback, personally. The maternal figure hovering over the patrons like a phantom saint loves to gab, so come with a sense of adventure, and refrain from supporting criminal behavior—she is a strong advocate of justice. One side note: They make a mean "old-fashioned." A couple of those, and you're on your ass. Nighty-night, you damned tourists.

The White Horse
1532 N. Western Avenue, Los Angeles
(323) 462-8088

Take It to the Stage!

Just a pissant and a dropkick from NBC Studios is one of the Valley's most infamous anomalies, where stage amateurs are treated like real-life professionals. It is a karaoke bar, called Dimples. Imagine the cast of *Days of Our Lives* breaking down a little Olivia Newton-John, or the dude who played Benson singing Sinatra, and you have a clear-cut image of this place. Or better yet, imagine hauling those precious lungs of yours, which sound so good in their natural bathroom environs, onto a stage before a most forgiving crowd; the acoustics are not nearly as good at Dimples, but hey, instant flattery from a drunken mass! They record your first performance for free (popping the virgin's cherry), and put you on television screens to overextend the sensation of being a star. And come with a sense of humor—not for the frail dude whose voice is cracking at every pitch, but for the "diehards" who come and hog the sign-up space. They are the bribers (greasing the host's palm for another song, just one more song!); the karaoke professionals; the narcissistic crooners with something to prove. They are *serious*, folks. And that makes for good comedy. Drink as if you are meeting the guillotine on the morrow. Karaoke is fun under those conditions, and addictive. And who knows, you might just get discovered!

Dimples
3413 W. Olive Avenue, Burbank
(818) 842-2336

Sweet-Potato Vodka and Sake—Together at Last

Away with geographical boundaries, welcome to New York City, California! If you're looking for the feel of Manhattan's Lower East Side bars in Los Angeles, pursue it no further than Vine, right next to the arty Villa Elaine apartment complex. There's no neon sign above the entrance to signify anything out of the ordinary, save a little green light. That green light means: "We are *the* discreet cool." In L.A., the current trend remains that no visible name on a bar means it will eventually have its run of catering to Hollywood celebrities, but don't let that dissuade you from going. Cover your blemishes with two coats of rouge, because the lighting is bright, but everything begins to fade when you get into the vibe of the vineyard. Vine is primarily a beer, wine, and sake bar, but they are innovative over there, *real* innovative. They have a variety of fondues to choose from (and the traces of Hollywood begin to reveal themselves) to stave off late-night hunger. And they have sweet-potato vodka, a Korean sensation that is taking America by storm, which is a sure sign of the organic times. The mixers are unique, including the mojito—a potato vodka drink with fresh mint leaves—and the signature sake-tini—a clever blend of sake and vodka, and a dash of vermouth, formed into a kind of martini. It is tiptop.

They also carry a wide range of vintage wines, and the regular stock of domestic and imported beers. This is a good place to discuss Buddhism, tantric sex, and yoga. Live DJs on the weekends.

Vine
1235 N. Vine Street, Hollywood
(323) 960-0800

I'm Your Private Dancer

Forget about throwing hard-earned cash down the thongs of slithery dancers. And don't look here for warehouse dance clubs with go-go boots and hair weaves: We haven't got that kind of info. But if you want lessons on *how* to dance, or want to get the thrill of shameless Frenchlike erotica without spending a paycheck in the pursuit, go to The Lava Lounge in Hollywood. Doorman Chris Rommelmann, originally from New York, stands in the entranceway and reenacts *Saturday Night Fever* every night, with a feathery dance-step despite his healthy frame. The night lights of Hollywood are his stars, and his hips swivel as light as a fishtail. He galvanizes the drunkards at the bar and in the dark booths to get out on the dance floor and shock their friends with chilling moves that have been collecting dust since their frat days. You'll feel alive the next day at work. Rommelmann is a seer. And he hasn't shame. His dance moves are closer to God than disco. He looks fluent when you're drunk or inebriated, either way. He is a dancing bouncer! But he is also a *heady* bouncer with athletic muscles. Must be 21.

The Lava Lounge
1533 N. La Brea Avenue, Hollywood
(323) 876-6612

Scratching's Okay

Hollywood Billiards has beautiful, lush green tables as far as the eye can see. . . . That's not exactly true, but this spruce parlor does have a lot of them. Falling somewhere betwixt a guy's spot (note the wooden bar, waitresses carrying big pitchers, and the big-screen TVs that play all the big NFL games on Sundays) and a perfect-date-for-the-adventurous bar and grill (the California-style pizza, the comforting green carpeting, good lighting), the Billiards has a hermetic charm unlike a lot of the regular L.A. pool dives; and a sort of underlying commercialism (the computerized jukebox seems to only have songs of the "Best of" variety) we don't always approve of. Still, for the economically unchallenged (rates range from $6 an hour to $13, depending on time of day, and day), it's a good place to spill some down, set some up, knock 'em back, and even miss a few times. For, unlike those dingier, more shark-infested places, this one tends to feel only as intimidating as your friends' living room, so more than likely they'll be the only ones who'll make fun of you when you scratch.

Hollywood Billiards
5750 Hollywood Boulevard, Hollywood
(323) 465-0115

Hair Music Ain't Dead Here . . . Hey, Isn't That Motorhead?

The last bastion of glam rock in L.A., this dirty little club doesn't even have bands anymore; but with all the hair and velvet around, you'll be sure to bump into somebody here who, if they didn't play for Warrant, at least they did a coupla tours as a roadie for them. Hell, you'll probably meet someone who sold drugs to Jimmy Page back in the day. You get the picture. This establishment, which was actually, at one time, a famous stop-off for bands like Mötley Crüe and even the Zep (dude, the Zep!), has kept it good and sleazy by still charging you ten bucks (hey, you wanna play, you gotta pay) at the door, which gets you two free drink tickets and not much else for your trouble. But, keeping in the vernacular—who gives a shit? The Rainbow's pizza is good and greasy and so are the framed pictures of your favorite rock heroes and other cheeseballs that line the walls. Oh, and we mustn't fail to mention that the girls are as slutty-looking as they come, just the way you used to like it—you, who once owned a Camaro and a Members Only jacket; you who once even had a band of your own. All of this is hacking (gotta lay off those cigarettes, dude) distance from **The Roxy**, **The Whisky**, and also a bunch of those pussy Sunset B-L-V-D clubs . . . as well as from the homeless guy who plays the bad-ass synthesizer in front of the Bank of America money machines (drop a dime and hear "Hey Jude")—not that you can afford to take any dough out since the record company has garnished your wages and you had to sell your equipment back to the Guitar Center to make the rent.

Rainbow Bar and Grill
9015 Sunset Boulevard, West Hollywood
(310) 278-4232

Michelle—Now, He Was a Real Pretty Girl

Michelle, a radiant six-foot-tall brunette with a sparkly dress and a stubbly chin, wanted to make sure we knew that his wife knew that he was in line at El Rey dressed like this. And Stephen, who looked exactly like David Bowie in his Ziggy Stardust phase, said he was working on a script about the life of Bowie. Ladies and gentlemen, and gentlemen and ladies and cross-dressers alike, welcome to Club Makeup, L.A.'s greatest, most extravagant, most lusciously fun glam-rock club, where the greatest in '70s, '80s, and yes, today's gender-bending music comes alive. But before we go on—please, as you're ushered through the front doors, don't forget to get your own free glam makeover, provided by the in-house stylists. A dash of red, a little yellow, some glitzy sparkles for maximum effect, and you're all set. And wait, over there, above you on the screen, do you remember that face? It's none other than Brian Eno, who made a splash with Roxy Music before moving on to his own ambient-music solo career. And there, on the next slide, that's Iggy Pop, looking tough but tender in his cheetah leather jacket. You gotta love him. Or how about him, the greased-down go-go dancer on the platform, over there, jiggling and sashaying to the Duran Duran song on the loudspeakers? Eyes away from the screen, folks, we have real life happening right before our eyes. And the band, featuring the female impersonating Alexis Arquette is just about to begin; so down a drink or two and make your way to the stage . . . and do be sure to secretly thank L.A. club promoters extraordinaires, Joseph Brooks and Jason Lavitt, for making all of your glamorama dreams come true.

Club Makeup
First Saturday of every month at the **El Rey Theatre**
5515 Wilshire Boulevard, Los Angeles
For more information, call (323) 936-4790
Or go to www.clubmakeup.net

Smoking Causes Fine Lines, Yes, but It May Be All Right at Beauty Bar

Though it's not an exclusive to this city (New York and San Francisco each have one), the Beauty Bar is nonetheless a pretty unique watering hole, which has, in past days at least, seen *the* proto-punk—Iggy Pop himself—inside its doors. And though as far as we know David Bowie hasn't made a guest appearance, the DJs here spin his tunes quite often. It all makes sense if you consider that Beauty, with its 1960s salon–style interior (complete with gigantic overhead hair dryers now used for seating), $10 drink/manicure deals, and backroom smoking area (a rare find in this new, smokingly correct town), is the epitome of glamorous decadence. Opened in February of 2000, the bar's beauty-school dropouts, as they are called, serve up a nice, stiff martini or the Platinum Blonde (Stoli, Malibu rum, and pineapple juice). For all you adventurous types, however, a decent vodka–energy drink mix will make you feel all bristly, like you did a line of coke in the bathroom before having a cocktail; that is, if you didn't already actually do a line in the bathroom, which no doubt the establishment frowns upon (though we think Pop might be proud).

Beauty Bar
1638 Cahuenga Boulevard, Los Angeles
(323) 464-7676

Strange Drinking

This place is an alternate universe seemingly created by a David Lynchesque deity. The nautical theme inside is strange enough, since the place is certainly more than twenty-five miles from the Port of Los Angeles. But wait. *Shhh.* Why is everything so quiet in here? *Clink*, go the glasses, as the sound of ice melting in its receptacle is nearly heard. A waitress, certainly not under the age of forty-five, wearing a young girl's skirt and tennies, delivers a fish-and-chips dinner to one of the tables. And who is that weird old man in the corner wearing a cravat and sipping his drink slowly, ever so slowly? Is this Lynchland running in slow motion, as well? It almost seems like it. But no! For there, at the booth, is a group of young hipsters, clanking glasses loudly and giggling. The weird solitude is instantly broken. Over there, a dude with bleached blond hair returns to his seat. "Man, that bathroom is weird," he says. And by god, he's right, as the H.M.S. Bounty is attached to the historical (but in need of a little work) Gaylord Apartments. One has to walk into its lobby and down into a basement maze to get to the toilet. Drunken trips to this strange dungeon are even weirder when you catch a glimpse of one of the Gaylord's tenants soberly carrying dirty clothes to the laundry room here. On the other hand, the drinks are cheap and the atmosphere, once you get used to the surreality, is warm. The booths are roomy; and somehow, over the years, the Bounty has become a favorite spot for the cool drinking crowd. So sail into this bizarre world if you get the chance—as the sign says, it's open every day of the year.

H.M.S. Bounty
3357 Wilshire Boulevard, Los Angeles
(213) 385-7275

Cops' Rear Ends

This secretive little dive—sans a defining signpost—is barely visible from the outside and, with its faux wood–paneled sweatiness, is not much to speak of from the inside. Yes, it has a pool table, a cramped little outdoor smoking cage in back, a dance floor, and plug-in fans that barely ward off the stuffiness therein. Come to think of it, The Shortstop is a pretty grim affair, despite its honest, bluish collar, poor arty clientele. Regardless, it seems to draw them in en masse on Fridays and Saturdays, which may have a little to do with its former life as a Los Angeles Police Department hang (and the general, grungy *Cheers* feel it does have). Yes, after the long days of hard work in the concrete jungle, many of our city's finest (though some would contest and say "worst") would come here to play darts, knock a few back, and, hopefully, not drive home drunk afterwards. The new owners haven't spruced up the bar's simple—how do we say?—ambience much; nor have they installed a much needed air conditioner (though DJs have been added to the mix). But most of us are happy to come here just knowing that the bar stools we sit on just may have held one of our Men in Blue's butts. (And speaking of butts, don't even *think* about lighting up inside here; it's illegal, don't you know!)

The Shortstop
1455 W. Sunset, Echo Park
(213) 482-4942

Canter's Is for the Peripatetic Living; the Kibitz Room Is for the Walking Dead

Founded in 1928, this kinetic little neighborhood gem of a kosher restaurant is packed day and night (just like the sign says, it's open twenty-four hours) with the various inhabitants of the Fairfax neighborhood, made up mainly of people ranging from the Orthodox Jewish to the young and hip. Take a number at the counter near the entrance, and there you'll soon have it, all kinds of baked goodies—or, at the deli bar, kosher-meated sandwiches and pasta mixes. Or kindly wait to be seated at one of the booths (conveniently equipped with phones) or tables and, once there, take a deep breath and raise your head to the sky to enjoy the chintzy (but strangely calming) fall-themed ceiling before you have to dive into the perplexingly well-stocked menu: peanut butter and jelly? They've got it. Thanksgiving dinner? They've got it (year-round). Matzo-ball soup? Of course. And it's good stuff, too.

Now, if hyper crowds of coffee-soaked entertainment industry types or scholarly diners ain't your thing, and liquid dinners are, you should probably be at Canter's adjacent bar, The Kibitz Room. Don't let the name fool you. This little rock dive—which, in better days, has seen such acts as Guns 'N Roses and the Wallflowers (notice the framed records on the wall) come through its doors—has settled into its depressingly delectable funk: Kudos to cheap tap beer and the local drunks who have made it so! On Sundays, a motley group of improv musicians leads in song while the slouching bar regulars and newcomers create their own brand of inebriated blues, service of the long-haired bartender (he plays in his own band—fittingly, we think, called Brown Ring), who's been there since at least as long as I've been in L.A. On other nights of the week, one can usually find local L.A. bands here, or the occasional DJ. On the way to the bathroom, a sad reminder of lost potential, hangs a yellowing picture of Hollywood's greatest male leads. Yes, some say that this great dive is the last stop before death, but we're optimistic about it: If you're here, you might actually be dead. Or maybe you're just in need of a big plate of Canter's fries, which can be delivered to your bar stool.

Canter's Fairfax Restaurant, Delicatessen, and Bakery
and **The Kibitz Room**
419 N. Fairfax Avenue, Los Angeles
(323) 651-2030

Art Deco and Old Hollywood Love

The Argyle Hotel, an upscale deco number protruding from the Sunset Boulevard skyline like a haunted Gotham City edifice holding the headquarters of some evil organization, is a little expensive for the nondiscerning. But you don't have to stay there to enjoy the overpriced drinks, food, and hors d'oeuvres at the hotel's Fenix Room. It's a small price to pay, really, for the experience. A couple of years ago this bar was the hottest spot in town, as young wannabes on lists waited in line for hours to catch a glimpse of celebrities like Hugh Hefner, who would occasionally show up with a bevy of nearly underage beauties at his side. As the hype has died down, the Fenix's class has not; and in fact, the establishment, a grand mixture of 1920s architectural ingenuity and the spirit of old Hollywood, can be enjoyed much more when it has some spare elbow room. The bar itself is a great place to sit and sip your hard-liquor drinks, but on a clear night (which is just about any night in L.A.), the best view is out at the pool. And though you may never feel quite like Garbo or Gable while out here enjoying the giant vista—you might feel like one of the Beverly Hillbillies as you lounge on a beach chair near the cement pond and glug down the finest in moonshine.

The Fenix Room at the Argyle Hotel
8538 Sunset Boulevard, Los Angeles
(323) 654-7100

Scary Fun

Once I was almost accosted in the restroom at Studio Café by an insanely drunken man slurring angry words, for no apparent reason, and wielding a bathroom key on a stick. I wasn't scared, though, because he was so soused, I think one deflective blow on my part would have knocked him off his balance onto the damp tiled floor underneath us. Yes, this greasy spoon attached to a bar/ karaoke club is always interesting, if vaguely scary in a Guns 'N Roses "Welcome to the Jungle" kind of way. The fact that I've been back since that first incident may indicate that I'm not really afraid of the place; though I'm not quite sure if that's true, either. Regardless of all that, the Café is always a good place for a drunken burger or tuna melt with some strange background conversation. (On one night, one old man told his friend about the music he wrote which was stolen by a certain famous singer.) And as for the karaoke—which takes place in the attached bar—well, it seems to be made up mostly of future dashed Hollywood dreams: fun in a tragic sort of way. But then again, one guy who used to sing Patti LaBelle tunes did go on to get a recurring part in *Buffy the Vampire Slayer*. I'm pretty sure his story is the exception to the rule, though.

Studio Café and Lounge
6633 Hollywood Boulevard, Hollywood
(323) 469-2139

Ahhh . . . the Balance

It takes a fine balance of cluttered ambience, good food, popular yet often pleasantly surprising music, and a good story to maintain the status of Best Dive Bar (and there are a goodly amount of them) on the beach. Hinano has all of these. Legend has it the original owner founded the bar in 1962 after he took a trip by 32-foot sailboat to Tahiti. There he discovered the local flavor and, more important, the eponymous Tahitian-made beer, Hinano. After consulting the brewery, he got the owners to agree to let him take both the beer and the name back to California. "They said, 'If you can get back to L.A., sure,'" said Mark Van Gessel, current co-owner of the place. Subsequently the sawdust-on-the-floor bar has shown up in scenes in such movies as *The China Syn-*

drome and *Falling Down*. Also, somewhere inside, Jim Morrison carved his name on the wall; it's still there today. The jukebox music varies from classic rock to new alternative to the kind that makes drunken pool players sway and go "Ahhhh." Meanwhile the beer is served in frozen mugs, the tuna melts and burgers are of the greasy, delicious variety, and, for the poor drinking sort, there is a free popcorn machine with paper tubs for self-service. In winter, a fire pit keeps the patrons warm in this entrancing atmosphere of beer merchandising, island flare, and surf lore.

Hinano
15 Washington Boulevard, Venice Beach
(310) 822-3902

Remember That Feeling?

Anyone from a place with actual seasons can appreciate walking into a toasty bar on a cold winter night and ordering up something highly alcoholic to warm up their frosty bones. Bigfoot Lodge, which obviously isn't in a city with actual seasons (unless you count as winter the two weeks of rain that L.A. gets around the holidays), kind of feels like this experience. This has a lot to do with the Lodge's pure rustic, cabin-in-the-woods feel. From its long oak bar, to its oversized, Lincoln Log–like walls, to the stone fireplace, to the cute Yellowstone Parkesque sign mentioning the Sasquatch, this quaint drinking room feels like the perfect hibernation spot from another six weeks of snow, sleet, and freezing rain. Maybe that's why the place packs all kind of folks, from rockabilly to punk to prep, into its clean, country gentlemen's (and women's) space on the weekends; or it could be the often-great music—it, too, running the gamut of tastes—spun on certain nights of the week. Whatever the reasons, this is a great place, if sometimes a bit too hip, to come to get out of the . . . uh, sun and smog.

Bigfoot Lodge
3172 Los Feliz Boulevard, Los Angeles
(323) 662-9227

RESIDENT TOURIST: LOS ANGELES

Keepin' Rock Alive

Besides having a separate, Plexiglas-walled smoking room that doesn't make tobacco users feel like anathema in this town, Spaceland—or Dreams and Spaceland, as it is formally called—is one of the best spots in town for good music, and we're not talking about the kind of ultratrendy lame stuff that makes up the brunt of bad radio in this town. No, the kinds of bands that play here are in fact usually of the underappreciated variety who, whether you are concerned or not, are doing their damned best to save rock and roll, even as it's dying before our very ears. Yes, it's a sad state of affairs, especially since Al's Bar, another L.A. rock-hard dive, recently closed its doors, leaving us faithful with one less good-rockin' home to lay our disenchanted hats. But Spaceland, which is nice and roomy (but also quite intimate with its pool table, video-game consoles, and long, comforting bar) is doing its best to be a part of the solution and not the problem. Maybe that's why, on almost any night there, you are likely to bump into a number of local musicians. (Once I saw Courtney Love's guitarist, Eric Erlandson, pop in for a round of Wiskey Biscuit, and heard later that the Circle Jerks' Keith Morris was in the front row.) We say, rock on, Spaceland. Rock on.

Spaceland
1717 Silver Lake Boulevard, Los Angeles
(323) 661-4380

Eastwood Drank Here—but So Did Bronson

Longing for a good old-fashioned steak house, with red leather booths, great Roquefort dressing, and cheese bread? Looking for a great old-timers' bar, where folks drink Bud and whiskey, and guns line the walls? What if they were the same place? Would you believe your good fortune? It's true—all this can be found under one roof at The Arsenal. Nothing fancy here, just good eatin' and drinkin'. The chateaubriand for two is a steal, and they carve it tableside, on a little table with its own lamp. Also featured are chicken and seafood entrées. It used to be just a little room, the restaurant consisting of about four booths and as many tables, with the bar on the other side of the place. They've since taken over space next door, and the newer space is more of a sports bar, but we really don't like to talk about that. It's those red leather booths, and some guy at the bar drinking scotch and milk because of his ulcer, that keep it real.

The Arsenal
12012 W. Pico Boulevard, West Los Angeles
(310) 479-9782

An Evil Foursome on the Club Circuit

If there's anything resembling a decent show at any of these three legendary clubs, *go*. They've all seen their share of history and played a major role in each chapter of the Los Angeles music scene, be it the 1960s, the punk rock of the late 1970s, or the Sunset Strip "hair bands" of the 1980s. The Troubadour is a fine showcase for touring bands-of-the-minute. (And who can forget when John Lennon stumbled in with a maxi pad taped to his head?) The Roxy shares a parking lot with the Rainbow Bar and Grill, a haven for has-beens, wannabes, and sometimes "actual" stars. Many people seem to have life chang-ing stories about seeing someone at The Roxy, and the sound is great. It's actually the place where *The Rocky Horror Picture Show* stage show made its debut on these shores. The Whisky—which of course gave the Doors, the Byrds, and Mötley Crüe their starts—and The Roxy are just a few blocks apart, and there's a bar or two in between them. One of them is the new Cat Club, which is said to have drawn the hermetic Axl Rose (former frontman for the defunct Guns 'N Roses) off the hill and back into society. And Duke's, the restaurant which used to

RESIDENT TOURIST: LOS ANGELES

be down on Santa Monica near the long-gone Tropicana Hotel, moved years ago to the same block as The Whisky, so there's plenty to keep you occupied on the Strip. Check the listings in the calendar section of *LA Weekly* for current lineups and upcoming shows.

The Troubadour
9081 Santa Monica Boulevard, Hollywood
(310) 276-6168
The Roxy
9009 Sunset Boulevard, Hollywood
(310) 276-2222
The Whisky à Go-Go
8901 Sunset Boulevard, Hollywood
(310) 652-4202
Duke's
8909 Sunset Boulevard, Hollywood
(310) 652-3100

Hops and Suds

Every college kid has thought of it, and somewhere it exists: "Suds," a combination bar/Laundromat. It'd be perfect, easing that evil necessity, laundry, with a brandy bumblebee. Well, I've yet to find "Suds," but these two places come close. The Universal Laundromat is a few yards away from The Casting Office, a neighborhood joint that ranks right up there with conceptual divinity. Not yet discovered by "the beautiful people"—thankfully—it's got some booths, a jukebox, and a small dance floor. Pop in your dark colors, come on over for a Cape Cod or an old-fashioned. Put 'em in the dryer, load up your whites, and wander back for a whiskey sour. When you're all fluffed and folded, have an Irish coffee while you wait for the cab that's been called for you. Remember, drink and dry responsibly (*wink*).

The Casting Office
3256 Cahuenga Boulevard, Studio City
(323) 851–4300
Universal Laundromat
3268 Cahuenga Boulevard, Studio City
(323) 850-0311

CHAPTER 3

Books and Coffeehouses in Los Angeles

Plenty of Coffeehouses and Bookstores Without the Corporate Stamp

Los Angeles is a far cry from Seattle; we get as much sunshine as they do rain. Under no circumstance does this mean L.A. is deficient in coffeehouses because, what, we lack a little precipitation? Come on! The bottom line is, we are addicted to caffeine nationwide, and coffeehouses—independent, good coffeehouses—are abundant these days. We have selected what we consider Los Angeles' most endearing coffeehouses in an effort to lessen the stranglehold the starfuckers have on us. We see the "green" Colombian-bean empire as a cancer growing outward from the murky Northwest. The coffeehouses listed below are our personal favorites, where the coffee and ambience are great.

As for the bookshops, same concept. We are trying to ease away from claustrophobic Borders. We highlight L.A.'s greatest bookshops, including the largest and oldest in the vicinity. The two components (coffee and books) seem to go hand and hand. Therefore, we have taken the liberty of grouping them together. It is perfectly understandable, and you would have done the same thing in our shoes.

Used Books, a Nice Kitty, and Acres of Minds

Acres of Books in Long Beach is not a cutesy name to give the average customer a sense of vastness, it is literally what the name says—a 13,000-square-foot book emporium! It is the second-largest bookstore of its kind, ahead of The Strand in New York City. Since 1934 Acres has been the haunt for a literature-hungry public and notable authors who are looking for a specific book. There are over one million books in stock: some used, some new, some vintage, some dating back before 1850, when Tolstoy was still a loose cannon. Is it any wonder that Acres was deemed a Cultural Landmark in 1991 by the city, or that enthusiasts, philologists of every discipline, and casual contemporaries from around the globe, visit the warehouse each time they're in southern California? Or that people ask for flashlights to search through the back fiction room for gems-in-the-rough? And hey—when you are hidden behind a stack of books and you see something scurry toward you, it isn't an oversized rat, but the Acres mascot, Penny the cat. Penny loves books. Her favorite book is *The Clown* by Heinrich Böll. Say hello, but refrain from using foul language. Penny won't have it. She is pure.

Acres of Books
240 Long Beach Boulevard, Long Beach
(562) 437-6980

Wake Up and Smell the Coffee

If the smell of fresh espresso beans invigorates your senses, or makes you feel slightly literary, then the Aroma Coffee & Tea Company and Portrait of a Bookstore, together at their Studio City location, is the hidden-away sanctuary for you. Three outdoor verandas surrounding an idyllic structure, with vines climbing the walls, and other assorted greenery, as well as stylish interior rooms, make one feel colonial and/or poetic. Portrait of a Bookstore, the name a spin-off of James Joyce's classic, sells everything from John Irving to Charles Bukowski, and has other merchandise for sale as well, such as stationery and New Age items, incense and diaries. At Aroma, some serious work can get done on that script you've been meaning to write, or that book you've been meaning to read. Or you can lounge with your friends, the smell of jasmine in the air, while enjoying a bagel and an uplifting café au lait. The back gallery is perfect for outdoor dining, with umbrellas and patio furniture, and the consistent golden hue from the ofttimes forgotten sun. It will make you regret that "green" chain coffee emporium, Star . . . something or other.

Aroma Coffee & Tea Company and **Portrait of a
Bookstore**
4360 Tujunga Avenue, Studio City
(818) 508-6505 (Aroma Coffee & Tea Company)
(818) 769-3853 (Portrait of a Bookstore)

First, There Was Vroman's

Friedrich Nietzsche, that saint among saints, was alive when A. C. Vroman started up his Pasadena bookstore in 1894, which seems alarming in the sense that it feels like Nietzsche lived a thousand years ago. Sure, the location has changed, and the concept has evolved, but hats off to longevity, right! Vroman's is intimate and clearly expansive (for a bookshop) at the same time. Employees have recommendation cards they fill out and hang throughout the aisles to give you a general synopsis of a book. This actually seems very appropriate in the quiet, bookwormy atmosphere at Vroman's. There are many signings and readings going on virtually every night (check the monthly calendar for details), and plenty of signed copies available of a given author's book long after the plane has left. Vroman's is more than a bookstore; it is also a coffeehouse, a magazine stand, a toy store, and a place for souvenirs, cookware, party supplies, stationery, maps, festive seasonal gimcracks, and office supplies. Plenty of audio books and postcards, too. Plus, it is right next to the Laemmle Theater, which shows independent and foreign films and avoids mainstream consciousness—what more could you want? Over one million titles are accessible at Vroman's, people, so break down your Borders.

Vroman's Bookstore
695 E. Colorado Boulevard, Pasadena
(626) 449-5320

Bindery, Rarity, and Literary Clarity

The Heritage Book Shop, Inc., on Melrose was at one time a mortuary. It is now a place to find rare books, to get your own prose bound to cloth or leather, to locate first editions or manuscripts, and to hear yourself think. The primary difference between the mortuary that it once was, and the bookshop that it has now become? The mortuary was louder. It was like a frat-house keg party compared to the opulent tomb that it is now. The books are deathly mute on their shelves, and encased in polished wood caskets. The employees are all voiceless, hardly stirring from their Macs, and verily emotionless. Their faces do not greet you unless you initiate something. Even the air conditioner is muzzled into a pleasant hum. When walking through the various halls in a pair of high heels, you will think yourself a parade of noise pollution, and feel just horrible for disturbing those sleeping books. But the place is not without charm. It has the feel of preservation and care. And it contains a seriousness that should attract those who are serious about locating a rare Blaise Cendrars, or a first-edition Walt Whitman, before *Leaves of Grass* evolved. Check out the upstairs gallery for autographed letters and documents by famous authors. The binding service is excellent, too, giving you the chance to protect prose so that your great-grandchildren can read it long after you have dissolved back into art.

Heritage Book Shop, Inc.
8540 Melrose Avenue, Los Angeles
(310) 652-9486

Hold On to Your Permanent Bliss

Vine Boulevard was, a long-time-ago, Pepper Tree Lane, and then Weyse Avenue years later, and now it is Vine Boulevard, which is what we were told at Bliss Art House Café by owners Stefan Lysenko and Marie Blom. And we believe them, irrationally, because their café is so damn cool, and one is apt to believe anything in the right surroundings. This place, which opened in February of 2001, is a splendid coffeehouse with all the romanticism of a Mac James sunset calendar painting, with nightly acoustic/folk music for atmosphere. Bliss is conveniently located across the street from the Hollywood Mental Health Center, oddly enough, and just down the street from the Vine DMV. The décor is elegant, the frequenters subtle, and the artwork hauntingly beautiful (rotating on a monthly basis). Bliss' sandwich menu is "legendary," with Henry Miller, Rita Hayworth, Man Ray, Lucille Ball, Orson Welles, James Dean, and the aforementioned Mac James all being commemorated in baguettes and brie and Black Forest ham. Their chai latte is nirvana (pre-Cobain). Bliss also has AA meetings daily from 2:30–3:30 P.M., because frankly, they care. BYOB at night with small corkage fee. Open seven days.

Bliss Art House Café
1249 Vine Boulevard (at Fountain), Los Angeles
(323) 962-2986

Geek Love

Hollywood has its true geeks, and I am not talking those poor bastard poseurs who wear the stylish thick-rims to mimic Weezer, nor the bone-skinny, unkempt artsy types who double as geeks to achieve their commercial goals. I am talking Internet-loving, dot-comsters who think of nothing but technology and Internet gaming and Net-war, anything that simulates, virtualizes, or computerizes our antiquated flesh. You know who you are! Welcome to Badlanz, an Internet gaming lounge and coffee bar. Badlanz is a spacious, comfortable forum for human beings to dive nose-first into machines, where they will meet, via miraculous Internet communities, like-minded souls with similar fetishes (whom they will then virtually blow away in cross-country games of Quake). The place has an elegance about it inside (outside, it is as unassuming as, say, your typical hip Hollywood bar), with thirty computers—all Pentium IVs with 19-inch monitors—set up in three rooms, along with a PlayStation2 center set up on a big screen with living-room couches. Some of the walls are painted in camouflage and others contain black lights, inspiring the feral beast within to vent any bound frustrations into the nether-nor of machines. The Badlanz environment is by far superior for logging computer time to the industrial giants out there, like Kinko's. At $5 an hour, you can't go wrong. Some nights there are DJs, and live LAN parties.

Badlanz
1602 N. Cahuenga Boulevard, Hollywood
(323) 464-LANZ

Battling Lights

San Francisco has the cultish City Lights bookstore, which is a leftover Beat Generation favorite still embraced by Lawrence Ferlinghetti and Michael McClure, who live in the area. Big deal! Los Angeles ain't no second-class citizen, yo! Let the Baybies have their bottle. We have Skylight Bookstore, formerly Chatterton's.

Let's do a quick comparison. This place is every bit as romantic in its warmth as City Lights, only it doesn't have an equally poetic bar next door. It *does* have the Los Feliz Theater, though. Advantage: *Push*. We have frequenting writers like Aimee Bender and Jerry Stahl in our neck of the woods, up-and-comers, clear thinkers, empiricists, popinjays with chips on their shoulders. They have their Beats and touristy stragglers, and the occasional bohemian harp player. Advantage: *Skylight*. They have a brilliant corridor of surrounding strip joints and red-lighters in the vicinity of City Lights, we have coffeehouses and healthy restaurants. Advantage: *City Lights*. At Skylight the readings feel intimate, the cashiers are caring, and the genres are clearly marked. At City Lights the cashiers are cocksure and hippie-yuppie, the smells are of patchouli and dead wood, and Chinatown is on you like a wart. Advantage: *Push*. Ah! They are erected on legendary past masters, pioneers from the fifties, literary giants, credible writing! We, on the youthful promise of quasi-comedic authors like yours truly, *Resident Tourist*. Advantage: *Skylight*. You see? Los Feliz has got City Lights licked down the line. Now, only if we could get a few red lights strewn into the area.

Skylight Bookstore
1818 N. Vermont Avenue, Los Feliz
(323) 660-1175

Hang On, Soupy—Soupy, Hang On!

Being a tourist on the Sunset Strip can oftentimes make you feel like a YIELD sign on the autobahn, because you feel that everything is in motion except for yourself. It seems as though you're missing out. But you're not, so buck up. After you have dined at one of those "look at me" sidewalk cafés, and you have exhausted the overpriced Whisky, Roxy, and Viper Room, do the right thing and spend an afternoon at Book Soup across the street from Tower Records. The twenty-six-year-old bookery (hey, look, the debut of an exciting neologism!) was founded by the legendary Glenn

Goldman and has 45,000 titles. Despite the despicable image of all those dolled-up mannequin-people roaming about in that area, try to remember that some of them *can* read, and some of them have a sense of culture. Book Soup has very limited walking/ perusing space in its aisles, being so abundantly overstocked with books and magazines and whatnot. In fact, they are stacked precariously high. It is a wonder no accidents have happened (though I am positive the employees have some stories). Dangling from the shelves are cards with employee choices and recommendations, bolstering certain authors that need the fan of persuasion. Everybody at Book Soup seems a busy-bee. Have fun looking for the registers, too, which hide behind stacks upon stacks of books. You can visit time and again without ever seeing the cashier. Outside, there is a newsstand for passersby, and attached to Book Soup is the Addendum, where real-life authors and writers read from their works regularly. Make sure to go upstairs and check out Mystery Pier Books (a bookstore) while there, for first editions of classic writers like Salinger, Faulkner, and Steinbeck. Free parking in the rear.

Book Soup
8818 Sunset Boulevard, West Hollywood
(310) 659-3110

Doo-wop, "Splish Splash," "Monster Mash," and a Vat of Frozen Caffeine

If you're craving coffee of the iced variety, you'll certainly have no shortage of Starbucks or Coffee Bean and Tea Leaf's to choose from. And the ice-blended mochas served at the CBATL and all the variations are delicious, and refreshing beyond reproach. But be creative. Skip those despots. If you're in the Valley, forgo the chain coffeehouses and head to Café '50s, conveniently located just south of the 101 Freeway on Van Nuys Boulevard near **The Barrel** (see chapter 2). They serve an ice-blended mocha cappuccino that is so worth the drive, it's not to be believed. First, let's start with the size. It's served in a tumbler that's got to be almost 10 inches tall. Topped with whipped cream, it's rich and thick, but definitely an iced-coffee drink, not a milkshake. And the price is only $3.25. Two of these could take care of a family of five, easy. It's worth the effort, wherever you're coming from.

Café '50s
4609 Van Nuys Boulevard, Sherman Oaks
(818) 906-1955

CHAPTER 4

Day Trips from Los Angeles

South of the City of Los Angeles

San Clemente is a beachside township worthy of a little attention. If you're in southern California, you've got to fully take advantage of what makes this such an oasis; two things are the beaches and the year-round great weather. No matter when you visit, you'll undoubtedly have beach weather to enjoy. San Clemente is about seventy-five miles south of L.A., and a straight shot down Interstate 5. With no traffic, you'll be there in just over an hour. There are several beachfront choices when it comes to accommodations, but The Beachcomber Motel is top of the list. It's been there for fifty years, and the seaside bluff location is all at once charming and breathtaking. It's not a big place, featuring twelve rooms, all with kitchenettes. The rooms have no phones or VCRs, which preserves the serenity all the more and they have spectacular ocean and sunset views, thanks to huge front windows. Each window is decorated sweetly with vines of different flowers painted around the frame. The kitchenettes are stocked with utensils, pots, pans, a microwave, fridge, and coffeemaker. This is especially important when kids are in tow, as most parents know, but it doesn't hurt the old budget to have the option of eating in. There's a fire pit, with wood provided, which is a nice segue from dinner to bedtime at night. This weekend should be all about moseying. After you arrive and check in, a trip down to the beach is in order. It's a vast expanse of beautiful sand, with a pack of surfers visible to the south all day, and into the evening. Spend some time walking, resting, wading—it's good for the soul! For lunch, walk across the street to Cassano's, which serves delicious pizza and great salads. Recommended is the Canadian bacon and pineapple, which is fabulous. That, and a huge house salad should take care of you until a fashionably late dinner.

After lunch, take a walk up to the Avenue Del Mar, for a taste of the beach life via shopping. Russel's Stationers has a great display window filled with all things shore. Seashell wind chimes, bags o' shells, dried starfish, pencil holders, mirrors; lots of fun little things to recall the smell of salt air. The Posh Peasant, a store full of antiques ("clutter for your nest"), and the Posh Peasant's Tea Room look inviting, and World Core offers apparel for the surf, skate, and snow crowd. Lots of beachwear everywhere, and one of the perks of shopping in a southern California beach town is finding swimwear year-round! The Beach Club offers a nice selection of sunwear.

La Coterra Market features homemade tamales and a wide menu of Hispanic treats. Grab a few tamales for a snack later. There's a special feel to a small beach town, and it's definitely awash on Avenue Del Mar. People are friendly and relaxed, and the whole town has an easygoing vibe.

Head on back to The Beachcomber, and have a glass of wine on your front porch, as the sun starts to set. Feel free to do nothing for at least an hour, just enjoying the vibrant evening colors.

Dinner should be at Fisherman's Restaurant, right on the San Clemente pier about a block away. It's a terrific dinner house with superb fresh seafood and chowder. Their specialty is the famous Family Feast, and you'd better be hungry. You can choose the Clam Feast, the Crab Feast, the Salmon Feast, the Lobster Feast, or several others. It comes with a bucket of clams or mussels steeped in nectar, chowder (red or white), salad, rice pilaf, and lots of delicious hot bread. It's a lot of food. Other fresh seafood is tasty as well, like the mahimahi, or the ahi tuna, and there's a basic kids' menu and full bar. Fisherman's Restaurant actually sits on both sides of the pier. One side is the bar and Oyster Bar where they shoo you when there's a wait, and the other side is the restaurant. The best views come from being seated outside, right over the water.

Next stop is the fire pit, overlooking the ocean, back at The Beachcomber, with a cozy fire and a nightcap. The crashing waves lull you to sleep, as do the trains that roll down the nearby track with regularity. In fact, there's a stop right there, at the entrance to the beach. Maybe take the train from Union Station in L.A., since you really don't need a car once you're in San Clemente, another freeing thing.

In the morning, start breakfast at Rick's Tropicana Bar and Grill. It's also a bed-and-breakfast, which is another option for accommodations. There's a gringo menu, with eggs and bacon and such, as well as some interesting other choices like the chorizo scramble and a huge breakfast burrito. It's served with a hot, *hot* green sauce, so use it with caution. After breakfast, and if it's Sunday, you'll find a Farmers' Market on Avenue Del Mar, with fresh fruits, vegetables, honey, nuts, plants, and herbs. It's a nice stroll for working off breakfast, as well as sampling some delicious organic produce.

It's a good time for a walk out to the end of the pier, too. It's an active pier for fishing, and at the very end you'll find Schleppy's, where you can enjoy a refreshing iced mocha and fill all your bait, tackle, and pole rental needs. Talk about filling a niche.

Checkout time is eleven A.M. at The Beachcomber, but you
may want to spend a little more time beachside, as it's just so beautiful and calm. You'll be heading back into the poetic chaos that is
Los Angeles soon enough, so enjoy the fresh sea air, for just a little
bit longer.

The Beachcomber Motel
533 Avenida Victoria, San Clemente
(888) 492-5457
www.beachcombermotel.com

Fisherman's Restaurant
611 Avenida Victoria, San Clemente
(on the San Clemente Pier)
(949) 498-6390

Rick's Tropicana Bar and Grill
610 Avenida Victoria, San Clemente
(on the San Clemente Pier)
(949) 498-8767

There's No Good Reason to Get Lost in L.A.

If you're lost and wasting gas driving around, say, Tulsa, looking for, say, a "Johnson Circle," we don't know what to tell you.
To be honest, if you don't have some kind of remote tracking system, the best we can suggest is that you calmly pull over and ask
the guy behind the counter at 7-Eleven, which may or may not
work. Either way, we wish you good luck. If you were searching
for a Johnson Circle (or a La Cienega or a La Brea, for that matter) here in L.A., however, our answer—provided we didn't know
it already—would be much more concise: Get your ass down to
the map store and buy a **Thomas Guide** already! These ingen-
ious and wholly comprehensive ring-bound street guides are a
must for anyone planning to spend time here or in Orange
County without a personal tour master. (Wake up, people, con-
trary to popular belief, some of us *do* work here in sunny California.) Sure, the Guide is a little more expensive than your average

city map, but then L.A.—an odd stretch of spread-out hotbed pockets and a bunch of suburban sprawl—is not your average city. Founded in Glendale, the Thomas Guide Company has made these superconcise street maps for West Coast cities for over eighty years. And because of their recent partnership with the Rand-McNally Corporation, you may, with any luck, soon be able to find that hard-to-find cul-de-sac in Oklahoma. But until then, you might just want to stick to the streets of L.A.

Thomas Bros. Maps & Books
521 W. Fifth Street, Downtown
(213) 627-4018

Outside of L.A.

Tropic of Pacific Coast Freeway

When planning a day or overnight trip to break the monotony of city life, you would be hard-pressed to find a more suitable destination than **Big Sur**, some three hundred miles north of Los Angeles. Big Sur has all of the veritable seclusion and natural wilds a person could ever hope to find anywhere in America—and the world, for that matter—virtually untouched by the advances of technology. The ocean is feral and violently white near the rocky shores, while the copper precipices on the rim, when meditated on, are fantastic for clarity. Tremendous redwoods line the Pacific Coast Highway, and the smell of pine rests easily in the air. There is whale-watching from the mountainous clifftops, incredible species of flora and fauna, and some of the most gasp-inducing sunsets you could ever behold. Big Sur's weather is a point of serious contention, though, varying from mild springlike days to thunderous wind and rainstorms, so violent as to close the only accessible road in—the Pacific Coast Highway. (If heading to Big Sur, it is advisable to call ahead for conditions beforehand.) There are numerous lodges, restaurants, campgrounds, and picnic areas to take it all in, namely the multipurpose **Nepenthe** (*Highway 1, Big Sur, California, 93920; [831] 667-2345*). This is a visitor's paradise, with info on the legendary history of artists in Big Sur, an incredible restaurant with a gorgeous outdoor patio and tremendous view, called Café Kevah, and the Phoenix shop, which features everything from jewelry, books, stationery, and musical instruments, to ceramics and clothing. Emil White, a longtime Big Sur resident and renowned painter, still has his house standing east of PCH, about a quarter-mile south of Nepenthe, now a temple to writers and artists who want to pay homage to his cult friend and fellow reveler, literary giant Henry Miller. The house today is the **Henry Miller Library**, which is essentially a museum/bookshop with artwork and rare editions of Miller's prose, along with performances, lectures, and exhibitions. Standing in the Henry Miller Library is like glimpsing into Miller's mind, with all of the influential writers and religions, philosophy books and artwork, films and movie posters related to the man himself. There are books by well-known authors such as Balzac, Céline, and Bukowski as well as lesser-knowns like Jean Giono and Mikhail Bulgakov, in addition to signed postcards and watercolors by Miller. Sparsely set about the front yard are beautiful pieces donated by many area artists and passersby, with wooden oversized chairs and the like. This is a fundamental stop for anybody in the arts seeking out inspiration through nature and the people for whom nature opened up potential. Big Sur also has great locations for surfers, fishermen, and mountain climbers. Thirty-five miles north of Big Sur are the more civilized, and perhaps equally mesmerizing, towns of Carmel and Monterey. Here all the provisions can be gathered for stays at Big Sur, along with further amusements such as the famous aquarium, Cannery Row, and numerous seafood restaurants of the highest caliber. The best route from Los Angeles to Big Sur is to take the 101 Freeway to San Luis Obispo, and then take the #1 Freeway (Pacific Coast Highway) from there. Along the majestic coastline you can stop to see sea lions or pull over for spectacular views of vitreous waters and crimson-toned sky at sunset. The drive is approximately six hours from Los Angeles, and three hours from San Francisco. The trying components of the obligatory city will seem worlds away.

From the Hot Plate to the Fire—Las Vegas

Think that Los Angeles is evil and its people are driven by the devil and most everything in Hollywood is pretentious, vain, and besmirched? Take a little trip northeast on Highway 15 to Las Vegas and watch the horns of L.A. transform into an unmistakable halo. We know that this is a common place for L.A. residents to visit, but this is a perception piece aimed to make you same residents feel better about your whereabouts. Las Vegas is outwardly hedonistic, and it loves to take proletariats' and bourgeois bastards' (like you) money at every turn. Just 275 miles from our heavenly city, this licentious body of transgression sits in a vast desert with inviting neon signs and the sky-beams of the Luxor. Prostitution is vaguely illegal in the city proper, and wholly embraced on the "outskirts." (Locals say that the **Chicken Ranch** is great.) Every conceivable place has a casino, and there are hotels, showrooms, amusement parks, and malls packed fancifully along the Strip. Most people— and senility has a lot to do with this—assume hunched positions at quarter slots and video poker. These people are the worst of the lot, and should *not* be trusted with money. They deserve the bashings they receive, wearing their neon yellows and mesh hats and thick mascara. If you have to gamble, play blackjack or craps, where at least you can narrow the odds with mathematics and a feeling of control. You will still lose, on the whole, but hey, evil is inevitably triumphant. For the 80 percent who come home lighter in the wallet, L.A. will look like the Bible Belt—real tame, like a kitten or a buckwheat pancake. On your way to Sin City, make sure to spit on the Zzxyx sign out there in the desert, for getting cute. And when you pass that thermometer in Baker, make bets with your friends as to what the temperature is. I usually do. It is a good kickoff to the impending thievery you will encounter, and might earn you some good cake coming home. Hint: Always bet over 90 degrees.

Las Vegas
"666 Vacancy Drive," Nevada
(Phone number is manifold, call any 900 number and it is Vegas)

Snowboarding, Skiing, Fishing, and Big Pinecones

One of the greatest things about Los Angeles is our relative proximity to everything. When somebody says from his sweltering Burbank estate, "I sure miss the snow and cold of home," *Resident Tourist* wants to slap him. Real hard-like, too; a slap that would leave a purple handprint. Just two lousy hours from Los Angeles is the high elevation of Big Bear City, a small community of mountain men, snowboarders, hikers, naturalists, and heliumsuckers. This is every bit as "Mayberry" as your damn hometown, maybe even more so. Bruce Springsteen would write an elevenalbum masterpiece if he spent a week here. In Big Bear City, people come from all over to ski, snowboard, hike, picnic, sail, fish, run, sunbathe, train (*see*: Oscar de la Hoya), and generally get away. A large blue lake is prominent in the town, where much of this activity takes place. Since the elevation is very high up, oxygen is thin, making the air seem light. The ski slopes are open mostly in winter, but there are fantastic restaurants to enjoy year-round, such as The Griddle, which serves up the largest portions of homemade pancakes this side of Tangiers. Big Bear also has an intimate little zoo which gets you up close with brown bears and wildcats. They don't respond well to human bantering, we learned; in fact, they look menacing when toyed with, but, never fret, they are behind fences. Big Bear has clear, cold air in the fall and winter. Instead of boohooing about the Winter Wonderland back there in the boondock, take a trip to Big Bear City and sit by a fireplace while icicles form on the windowpanes. You never had it so good.

Big Bear City

Highway 10 east to 330 north. Follow signs to "Mountain Resorts" from there, or visit www.bigbear.com for information.

For Peace and Quiet and Concentration. You know . . . the Things You Need to Read *Ulysses*

Point Dume is just the kind of place you bring a date to neck with a little, on an isolated rocky beach. But slow down, reader, one thing at a time. The beach is essentially a protruding rock that juts out into the pond like a knot on a rapped forehead. You reach Point Dume from the Pacific Coast Highway, past Pacific Palisades, and farther north than Topanga. There is a sandy beach called Westward at the bottom of Point Dume, where people can sprawl out like bacteria and menace one another with flying disks and racket. Drive up the meandering hill, and you will get to the respectable Point Dume, where your lover will likely want to do more necking and stuff. Hold off! Park and make your way down the pathway to the waters below, and enjoy the optimum seclusion of, say, some place like Corfu, Greece. Once you're at the bottom, take advantage of the low tide by snorkeling and spearfishing. Lots of people do it, and it looks entertaining. Or simply walk along the rocky bottom of the beach, just necking away with your partner. No dogs allowed.

Point Dume State Beach

Off the PCH near Zuma Beach

Money Stolen and Unsolicited Crotch-Grabbing

"Push it. Push it, Push it," the friendly man trying to help me with the ATM machine said in his thick accent. "Now push in the numbers." I did, feeling slightly guilty trying to hide them from his view. And when my card spit itself back out without giving me money, falling on the floor, the nice man picked it up and handed it back to me. Strange, the Good Samaritan disappeared quickly after giving me back my plastic chip.

It wasn't until about half an hour later (and numerous failed attempts at other machines) that my friend suggested I look at the card. No, that wasn't my name on the card, and yes, by the time I got hold of my bank to cancel *my* card, the nice man had gotten away with $300 of mine.

Out came the credit card and on went the night. In a drunken haze we wandered into a dirty strip club where the girls felt no shame sitting on our laps and grabbing for our packages. (Oddly, these girls ignored our female companion, never asking if she was a girlfriend. She wasn't.) Despite our buzzes, Bill and I walked out with embarrassed visages; fun, but too much—it all was. On the way home Bill pulled out a shopping list made by his friends: on it, requests for a whole bevy of painkiller brands and psychiatric medicines. A quick stop at one of the open-all-night pharmacies, some stuttered Spanish on Bill's part about all his pains, and Bill became his friends' "Doctor Robert." "Give me one of those," I said to Bill as we made our way back to the car.

Yes, Tijuana, that dusty little border town, is a grungy palace of sin, unlike even the worst parts of L.A. But if you can turn a world-weary eye away from all the poverty and keep a strong (stronger than mine) grip on your wallet, you're sure to have a decadently delectable time. The beer and tourist goodies are cheap and the bars are open all night. And Americans are welcome to stay seventy-two hours without a visa (but try to have your passport near you at all times). Another suggestion: Park your car on the American side and walk over, lest you end up having to bribe a cop—we've heard stories, believe us—to get it "unstolen" for you.

Tijuana
(I-5 all the way south of the border)

Not Quite Santa Barbara, but Not Quite Columbus, Ohio, Either

Ventura, about one hour north of Los Angeles, combines a delicious small town demeanor with the calm freshness that permeates a beach community. It's a straight shot north on Highway 101, and makes for a quiet break in the bustle of L.A. Exit the 101 at California Street, and head east. About two blocks later, park. Parking is plentiful and free, but keep an eye on the clock, as there are time limits. Start with Main Street, which is the main street. Did we say small town? It's jammed with antique stores, second-hand places, curio and collectible shops. Looking for a pink princess phone, refurbished and ready to go? Found one here, complete with a one-year warranty. The Humane Society Thrift Store is always a good bet for a purchase, as is Frank's Furniture. The Nicholby Antique Mall is crowded with booths from different vendors, and you'll have a wide selection to browse. You'll find lots of furniture, which may not be convenient if you're traveling, but the prices are generally so reasonable that even if you have to ship something home, it'll be a good deal. You don't have to venture off Main Street, as pretty much all the good stuff sits right there, within about five blocks. Oak Street might make you veer off for a minute, with a couple of interesting collections and a Goodwill Industries Thrift Store as well. Time for lunch? Got kids? Head into the Busy Bee Café, a '50s-themed diner with something for everyone. Chili burgers are always a good bet, and the milkshakes are definitely worth the splurge. There are plenty of cafés and coffee places, if you're just interested in a little snack, rather than a full-on lunch. For dinner, you absolutely, absolutely must dine at Rosarito Beach Café. It's simply some of the best food I've *ever* eaten. Handmade flour tortillas (made right in front of your eyes) served warm that melt in your mouth; a special quesadilla of the day; and fresh fish prepared any one of five ways. Try halibut, Yucatán-style, with a paste of achiote seeds, citrus juices, and spices; or Veracruz-style: green olives, capers, tomatoes, and onions. And have the salad with the house dressing, a tangy orange/chile blend, sweet and sharp. Rosarito Beach Café alone is worth the drive. But definitely make it dinner. The lunch menu is limited and you get chips instead of those delicious tortillas. The beaches in Ventura are beautiful, and you'll be able to stretch out and relax. Parking structures are conveniently located next to the beach, and the Ventura Pier offers a nice vantage point north and south, as well. A clean stretch of sand beckons you as the waves roll in. There's a snack shop on the pier, because swimming sure can make you hungry.

Rosarito Beach Café
692 E. Main Street, Ventura
(805) 653-7343

Forget the Mugs and Posters: Get in the Car

Any guy who has left his house with tousled hair, any girl who has fallen in love with such a guy, anyone who has thought about how cool smoking looks, anyone who has looked in the store windows along Hollywood Boulevard or in any poster rack across the United States, can certainly attest to the lasting image of James Dean. He was, and he remains, the quintessential image of reckless, misunderstood beauty, and rebelliousness. And, for that matter, a martyr to merchandising, whose images are no longer owned by his deceased self, but to the James Dean Foundation Trust, a corporation that jealously guards (and has filed the occasional lawsuit in doing so) Dean's image—to be, of course, turned into cheap mugs, T-shirts, and the like. But don't get us wrong; we're all for marketing. (And as a matter of fact, we plan on buying the HOLLYWOOD sign from the money we make from this book; we'll then turn around and sell the sign's photo rights to the highest bidder.) Still, for all you real fans of Dean's work, we suggest that instead of paying at his altar, you *pray* to it. How, you ask? Head east, young man. That is—if you're morbidly inclined enough—take a day trip following the path he took in his Porsche Spyder on that fateful day in 1955, which left him dead as a result of his inclination toward speed. Please do be careful, though.

James Dean day trip
For more information go to:
www.americanlegends.com/jamesdean/facts/lastride.html

CHAPTER 5

Exercise and Parks in Los Angeles

The Shame of Jazzercise and the Emergence of New Styles

L.A. just may be the only city in the United States that featured a TV news story on how city folk here are coping with the September 11, 2001, attacks by doubling up on their efforts at the gym. And I, for one, am a little ashamed of us on that front, especially since the newsman who presented the story, and the people he interviewed, talked about this without the slightest hint of embarrassment, as if flagrant vanity were a universal thing in uncertain times. Yes, in many ways we are a city of silly fools, sometimes led by a group of fearless buff celebrities utilizing a combination of dieting and intense sessions at Crunch to stay healthy-looking. (Though some of these trend-conscious folks have begun to tout the virtues of more low-impact exercises such as yoga.) We can't in all good conscience advise you to go looking for these sorts at the local fitness hot spots, though other tomes may suggest it.

But of course, even though L.A. has turned the fitness business into an often scarily disgusting industry made up of self-help pop psychology and fad diets, we still don't deny that the rest of the world (with the exception of possibly most of the South and all of France) likes to feel healthy. We just don't think you need to pay $15 single-day fees at 24-Hour Fitness to stay in shape when you visit here. And *please*, people (we feel we have to say it again), don't go try to find Brad Pitt at Gold's Gym; he wants to be left alone to his three sets of biceps curls in these harrowing times.

Now, if you're still full-on set on staying sporty—which we *don't* advise against—while visiting our city, there are plenty of good outdoor (yes, *outdoor*; you know, "sunny California" and all that) alternatives to choose from.

Runyon Canyon, for example, boasts not only a rigorous climb to the top of a hefty peak, but is also hands-down the best damn view in the city. From the highest point, and on a clear day, one can see everything—and we mean *everything*—in L.A.: from downtown to the Sunset Strip; yes, even the ocean if you squint your eyes just right. The view is literally amazing and has no doubt inspired many the aspiring actor to think to him or herself, *Someday this will all be mine.* Adding to this, those stalwart souls willing to go the extra mile can, from Runyon, make their way as far as Griffith Park and the Observatory, where that dancing knife-fight in *Rebel Without a Cause* was filmed.

Just over the Valley, in Studio City (take Laurel Canyon to Fryman Road), is **Fryman Canyon,** another blood-circulating hike up to a peak where, from the top, one can see much of the strip-mall hell that is San Fernando Valley. And though it is not necessarily *the* place to bring autograph books, one can often see the occasional low-level movie star or TV actor hiking here—along with the rest of the plebians. For example, we once saw Ed Begley Jr., actor and energy activist, hopping into his electric hybrid car after his brisk Sunday-afternoon Fryman trail walk.

A lower-impact deal can be found in the **Silver Lake** area at the L.A. Reservoir, which has a paved sidewalk encircling it, making it a good bet for walkers of the leisurely variety. And sure, the beaches (especially Venice, with its smooth bike trail leading to the Santa Monica Pier) are always a good place to get a run or Rollerblade in, but even better are the many canyons and winding trails that Malibu and Ventura—just over the country line—have to offer.

Barring these activities, one can always catch a pickup game of basketball (see listings below) or take a flying leap into the ocean or into one of the many L.A. public pools.

Pickup Artists on the Basketball Court

Looking for a good pickup game of basketball? Want to show that the new Air Pump low-tops added four inches to your vertical? Like shooting off the window from twenty feet? Well, *Resident Tourist* has a couple of places you can go to compete with solid play-ahs from all walks. If you can dunk the basketball, then you are more suited to **Rogers Recreation Center** on Eucalyptus Avenue and Hyde Park Boulevard in Inglewood. The competition here is steep, and these gents take their game seriously. Other places for solid competition are **Centinela Park** at Prairie Avenue, also in Inglewood; and the **Westwood Recreation Complex** (1350 Sepulveda Boulevard, on Wilshire at Ohio Avenue). If you just want to run but don't necessarily have Nick Van Exel hands, try the **Hollywood YMCA** for daily pickup games and **Lincoln Park** in Santa Monica. Or go to **Hazeltine Park** in the Valley (in between Van Nuys Boulevard and Hazeltine) and see juvenile parolees mixing it up with anything from trash-talking high schoolers to elderly ex-college types. Hell, the Clippers sponsor the courts there, and the nets are always on the rims. Dish the rock. Don't hate.

Run, Beast . . . Run!

Tired of watching from your damn couch as the Kenyans effortlessly blow past the rest of the world in marathons? Seeing red? Want to do something about it? Well, then, you need to start training, chubs. Your first stop—and pay attention, because this is mandatory—is Phidippides in Encino (open since 1980), a marathon runner/trainee's paradise, where the employees take the time to find the right shoes and accessories for your anticipated overthrow of those pompous Kenyans. Co-owner Craig Chambers literally ran to work for five consecutive years in the 1980s, which is the equivalent of a marathon every single day, at twenty-six miles round-trip from the Santa Monica mountain trails to Encino. Based on that alone, he qualifies as an in-store expert. At Phidippides, they fit you into the right shoes for your gait, and give pointers on how to train, how to set and achieve goals, and how to make steady progress. And, most important, they *encourage* you with their positive attitude. The place is unassumingly located on Ventura Boulevard, but it has an impeccable reputation for those who are serious about running, training, walking, and general exercise. Gotta run!

Phidippides
16545 Ventura Boulevard, Encino
(818) 986-8686

Domesticated Funplex with All the Amenities

Fun for the whole family, the Pickwick Center has twenty-four lanes of bowling, an ice-skating rink, an arcade, six banquet rooms, and, to attract the public extremists, romantic gardens for tying the knot. This is one of those places where ex–varsity football fathers go to keep their competitive edge; mothers go for bragging rights over other women of similar age; kids go for their first taste of Midwestern sport and spirit. And there is no lack of beer. What I mean is, the bowling leagues are fiery affairs, with lots of tension and expectation. On-premise merchandise sales consist of custom bowling balls with fancy images, like green-and-red-dragons, ABA "basketball" bowling balls, and Winnie-the-Pooh. Cute stuff, for sure. The ice-skating classes range from freestyle to foxtrot, expressing the highbrow swanlike grace that we strive for in elderly life. And hockey leagues are run through Pickwick, where all the aforementioned components combine. But fret not—all is not league-oriented. This is a public fantasy-land as well. Children can get lost in the labyrinth of banquet halls and gardens and arcades and cocktail lounges, so be careful. Adults have a more precise mission, but succeed in forgetting the forty-hour humbug with all the bustling activity. Fun, *fun*! Pictures of very domestic people align the walls, and waltz music is heard near the ice. Pickwick is available for private parties, with on-campus accommodations available. Call for info, or check out the Web site at www.pickwick.com. The Web site is more modern-looking than the facilities are. Who cares? This place would be good for Salvador Dalí to further push the surrealism envelope.

Pickwick Center
921 W. Riverside Drive, Burbank
(818) 842-7188 (ext. 350, or 351 for directory desk)

These Weren't Milwaukee's Best

If you come to Hollywood carrying a 239 bowling average along with your noticeable Wisconsin accent, you have a Midwest beer/cheese gut and/or a toupee, and you rightfully consider bowling *exercising* (God bless you!), go check out Hollywood Star Lanes; you will soon discover that *nothing*—including the once predominantly and mandatory body weight of two hundred pounds and over—is sacred. This place is inhabited by youthful, firm-bodied model types who have fashionable bowling shoes and skimpy outfits. They bowl an impressive 120 or thereabouts every game, which is genuinely lauded in their circles. And they have perfect teeth. Their skin is pulled back on their faces, without a trace of multiple chins; no crow's feet on their eyes! They smile a whole bunch, and talk about pseudo-artsy things. It is all about glamour on the lanes these days; one more nerdy/cool activity they've snatched from our buffalo-winged jaws! These people deserve punishment, the dumb bastards, and it could come at the hands of yourself. Go head-to-head with them in the alley, defeat them, call them "snot-nosed punks," grab their girlfriend's ass, etc. Take back what is fitfully yours, elder bowler. These pip-squeaks are worth nothing but a 7–10 split, which you picked up a thousand times back in Sheboygan. Plus, for those bumpkins who get off on movie locations, they filmed some of *The Big Liebowski* right here. There is a bar, a café, and a riveting video arcade for non-bowlers. Hollywood Star Lanes has some cheap specials for just practicing, like $5 for three games on designated nights. Call for info.

Hollywood Star Lanes
5227 Santa Monica Boulevard, Hollywood
(323) 665-4111

Who Needs Integrity When You Can Revert into Monkeydom?

When I told my musician friend, Stan Bolinowitz of the band Staff, about my escapades at Corbin Bowl in Tarzana, he took it to heart and wrote a touching if not uplifting number that he called "The Great White Trash." It was, and still is, his opus. Let me inspire you, too, reader. Corbin Bowl is a life-affirming bowling experience that will have you questioning your resolve the morning after, while nursing a cheap-domestic hangover. They have the momentous midnight rock-and-roll bowling thing that became hip outside our fair city, with the loud music and light show. That's a given. But they also have a sports bar inside, where white-hot karaoke goes on each weekend, and people pour their hearts into a microphone to the tunes of the B-52s and Credence

Clearwater Revival. Here's where problems start: With the prospect of cheap drinks, and those "Am I good enough" unsettled nerves, sobriety becomes a finite proposition. It's curtains from here, because you mistook that little Rod Stewart performance of yours as something special. And then you go throw drunken gutter-balls down the alley, or use the child rails like a jackass, and you curse, kick, scream, and harass total strangers and beleaguered friends all in the name of revelry and fun. The morning after is an ominous fog, and you swear you won't do *that* again. *Getting so shitty at a bowling alley? What was I thinking?* you will ask. But once the headache subsides, and the morning-shower song isn't enough, and the prospect of bowling a perfect game dominates your spirit . . . you'll be back. They *always* come back.

Corbin Bowl

19616 Ventura Boulevard, Tarzana

(818) 996-2695

This Ain't ESPN

Sports Center Bowl is high, *high*-end. It's ritzy, it's shiny, it's space-age hip. Potted plants dot the lanes, a bright mural adorns the wall where the alleys run, and the arcade is huge. The arcade houses pool tables and loads of high-tech games. Friday and Saturday nights feature Rock & Bowl, when they turn the lights down and the music up. Flashy colored lights can be a little disorienting when you're trying to pick up that 7–10 split, but loud music adds a lot to your game. And Sports Center is directly connected to Jerry's Famous Deli and its huge menu, with more choices than you could possibly need. The big portions don't come cheap, but it's delicious. Both bowls have birthday packages for kids, and Sports Center's are quite extensive, with options including food from Jerry's Famous Deli and accessories such as trophies, jewelry, snow globes, candles, and even the invitations.

Sports Center Bowl
12655 Ventura Boulevard, Studio City
(818) 769-7600
Rock & Bowl
Fridays after 9 P.M.; Saturdays after 10 P.M.

Bird-Watching Watching

The signs read "BEEWARE" when you're strolling through the serene nature trails of Descanso Gardens—and they ain't just pulling your chain. If you're a daredevil (and if you've spent money on this book, you definitely are) who feels most alive when confronting danger, go there. The bees are one of many hazards resting over this peaceful park like a storm cloud. Sure there are bees, thousands of them in the rose garden alone. That's easy to spot. Other dangers are less conspicuous. Like poison oak! And spiders, lots of spiders. And bats, cacti, columbine (probably innocuous, but the name carries a sense of foul play), coyote, potential walls of mud, and a perpetual rustling in the nearby bushes. (None of these will attack you unless provoked.) Of course, these are all a part of the natural habitat that makes up one of the most gorgeous sites in southern California. Descanso is an excellent place for bird-watching and photography. It is also a grand place for watching bird-watchers and practiced ornithologists, and spotting some rare old birds of a different feather. For instance, when I was there, I spied an eastern blue-hair with binoculars (*z'tourist imbecili*), and a nimble khaki with telescope (*eruditis quidnunx*), both of which disappeared when I phoned *National Geographic*. They are there by the gaggle, somebody told me. Descanso's highlight is the tiny-train ride through the gardens. It is a chance for adults to be children and for children to see yet more magic in their boundless perceptions of things.
Descanso Gardens
1418 Descanso Drive, La Canada-Flintridge
(818) 952-4400

I Saw the Greatest Men of My Generation Turned into Rocks

Arcadia, a known side-project of those 1980s spotlight-hoggers Duran Duran, was a cool-enough name as to inspire a whole town, just outside of Pasadena. Don't know much about it outside of that, except that the Los Angeles Arboretum is located there. This is a huge, 127-acre continental garden, heavily mani-cured and particularly green, that takes a good couple of hours to conquer by foot. Historical landmark number 367, the Queen Anne Cottage (built in 1885) is there, which is phenomenally eerie with its smiling mannequins and taxidermy and ghostly antiquities. Yikes! But wandering around the place are peacocks, geese, and ducks of all gender, most of which are passive and quite hungry (be sure to bring some feedings for them to test their temerity). There are spectacular ponds with lilies, turtles, frogs, and stranger birds like the South American ibis. But the specialty of the Arboretum is the gardens. The Kallam Garden, Meadow-brook, where the base of a magnificent waterfall rests, with all kinds of perennials and annuals, is an excellent place to paint a picture, or to recline and talk about Marxism. There are also trop-ical greenhouses with multiple bromeliads and ferns, and African, Australian, and Asiatic sections to take in, along with a 26,000-volume library, a gift shop, Lucky Baldwin's manse and lagoon (where television's *Fantasy Island* was shot) and a café (aptly called The Peacock). Check out the white floss silk tree (Peruvian), and tell me that thing is not set to birth a small copse of infant trees. It is pregnant, miraculously. And the greatest men of history are nothing more than stones, like Hal Compton, who now rests under a soft bush as a hunk of granite. Open daily, 9 A.M.–5 P.M. Admissions close at 4:30 P.M.

The Arboretum of Los Angeles County
301 N. Baldwin Avenue, Arcadia
(626) 821-3222

The Pooch on the Free Range

Okay, so this one's not such a secret to residents, but it's still worth a visit, whether you're traveling with your dog or not. It's sure to be a break from the crowds and hustle of sightseeing. Hundreds of happy dogs and their chatty owners fill this park daily. There's the guy with the three golden Neapolitan mastiffs lumbering around the perimeter. Whippets are a lot of fun to watch, as they careen around. And you never know who may pop by. Chrissie Hynde and Alicia Silverstone have been observed enjoying the hounds. There's a playground and fenced-off play area for the kids. And everyone has such wonderful etiquette. I've seen the crowd turn en masse on a guy with an aggressive German sheperd, and he was forced to leave. Everyone picks up their own poop, ensuring a pleasant day for all. There's a snack cart to refresh, and low-cost vaccination clinics once a month, to make sure you're up-to-date on shots. Public Service Plea: Please get your dog spayed or neutered, especially if you take him to parks like these.

Laurel Canyon Dog Park
8260 Mulholland Drive, Studio City
(818) 756-8060

Doing It Doggie-Style

It's a big, flat, securely fenced field in the heart of the San Fernando Valley. Located at the corner of White Oak and Victory, it's dotted with trees, which is essential in the summer, and has a little separately fenced half-acre spot for small or timid dogs, which must be a welcome relief from the excited, rambunctious pooches on the other side of the fence. As with most of these dog parks, low-cost vaccinations are offered on-site. Call for schedules.

Sepulveda Basin Off-Leash Dog Park
17550 Victory Boulevard, Encino
(818) 756-8190
Also:

Silver Lake Recreation Center
1850 W. Silver Lake Drive, Silver Lake
888-LAPARKS (6 A.M. to 10 P.M.)
Westminster Senior Citizens Center
1234 Pacific Avenue, Venice
888-LAPARKS
(This one's a bit smaller, just shy of an acre, but has a separate area for small dogs.)

Charles Bronson and the Bat Caves

Once a working rock quarry for the Union Rock Company, the Bronson Caves are a favorite spot for filmmakers, both big-screen and television. You might recognize them as Batman's Bat Cave, or from the earthquake scene in *Short Cuts*. Take Canyon Drive, off Franklin in Hollywood, all the way north to what is a western entrance to Griffith Park. Park in the small lot and head back to the utility road about 200 feet down to the left. Hike about a quarter mile on the dirt road and as you take a turn to the left, there they are. It's very secluded and you don't want to be alone. It is, let's say, *atmospheric*. It's quiet, and the scrub along the hills is blowing, and the only sound you hear is the crunching of the rocks under your feet. Walk through the cave, and on the other side you'll come out to a landscape that looks nothing like Los Angeles. It's clear why it's a favorite filming spot. It can be another planet, or the Ponderosa, for all the audience knows. Another prime viewing spot for the HOLLYWOOD sign, as well.

Bronson Caves
Canyon Drive, Hollywood Hills

Andy Griffith? Nah. Well, Maybe. Who Knows.

Griffith Park is huge, with many entrances all over town. It's actually the largest municipal park and wilderness area in the entire United States, with just over 4,100 acres. It features areas like Fern Dell, off the Western Avenue entrance, and a bird sanctuary up Vermont Canyon Drive. It's home to the Greek Theatre, an outdoor amphitheater that is a great place to see music during the summer. There's the Gene Autry Southwest Museum and across the parking lot, the L.A. Zoo. For the kids, pony rides and covered-wagon rides—found near the Los Feliz Boulevard/ Riverside Drive entrance—along with the Griffith Park Southern Railroad, will keep them amused. Farther into the park, at Park Center, is the famous Griffith Park Merry-Go-Round, sur-rounded by acres and acres of grass, playgrounds, and picnic tables. The Griffith Observatory will be undergoing a huge renovation and expansion from January 2002 to late 2004. Unfortunately, it will be closed to the public during that time, but expect quite a to-do when it finally reopens.

And furthermore:

Even without the Observatory, You Learn Something New Every Day

In the beginning of 2002, the Griffith Park Observatory, that beautiful dome wherein a gigantic telescope and many public exhibitions are housed, closed its doors for a much-needed reno-vation. So, at least until 2005, you won't be able to watch Fou-calt's Pendulum prove that the Earth rotates or see eruptions on the sun's surface, nor, for that matter, will you ever be able again to drop acid and check out the famous laser show there (though, as we speak, the Laserium is looking for grander digs for what will be an updated version of their music/light show, so check www.laserium.com frequently for updates).

However, you can still garner your lessons on the land around where the observatory sits. Here's how you catch a crawdad for example: First, take a piece of string and tie it to a stick to form a provisional fishing pole. On the end of the string, tie a little piece of meat (hamburger, pork, anything will do). Then, dip the string into water. When the crawdad sees the meat, he'll grab it with his claw and you can yank him out of the water, put him in a water jug, and take him to keep as a pet or, heck, why not, to eat.

I learned that one day whilst walking through the Griffith Park, the 4,100-acre area of lush, green lands and earthy hills originally donated by mining magnate Griffith J. Griffith way back in 1896. Quite a few folks had their poles dipped into the little streams that run through the place, and after curiosity succeeded in conquering me I went up to one of these "fishermen" and held a stunted conversation—he spoke Spanish—with him to find out what was going on. Afterward, I took a brisk hike up past barbecuers, frolicking kids, and lovers up to the land where the observatory sits. I came back down the other way, passing by the Greek Theatre, a large concert auditorium, which gets many of the mid-size to big acts that come to L.A.

And as I made this trek, I also learned that the park is home to plenty of critters, including sun-lounging lizards, tiny rodents, and snakes, one of which I saw slowly slink its way up the side of a steep hill; and on the way down the paved road leading to the telescope, I also learned another thing: this is a brisk walk. And I'm out of fucking shape.

Griffith Park Observatory
2300 E. Observatory Road, Griffith Park
(323) 664-1181 or (213) 665-5188

Hollywoodland Park Has Curvy Roads That Make Us Say, "Whee!"

This serene spot offers not only a terrific view of the HOLLYWOOD sign, but an equally terrific view of the southwest Hollywood Hills. It also takes you around Lake Hollywood, the reservoir. And please drive carefully, as the surrounding road is a favorite for walkers and joggers, often with strollers. Off Barham Boulevard, make a turn onto Lake Hollywood Drive. Lake Hollywood Drive winds to the left, then to the right, at which point you'll make a left onto Wonder View, which has a stop sign. A quick jog right and you're back on Lake Hollywood Drive, with the reservoir in view.

Follow the curvy road around the lake, keeping a careful eye out for the aforementioned joggers. Make the left onto Tahoe Drive and up the hill to Canyon Lake. About 100 yards up, you'll see a vast expanse of grass, with a fenced-in play area tucked into the corner, surrounded by picnic tables and benches. Dogwise, it's officially an "on-leash" dog area, with signage directing you to other, "off-leash" areas—so beware. It's quiet, and rarely crowded, surrounded on all sides by hills covered with scrubby brush and fabulous homes, including the infamous Madonna/Bugsy Siegel house, with its vivid brick and yellow colorings. A nice respite from Hollywood, without losing touch with it.

Hollywoodland Park
Canyon Lake Drive, Hollywood Knolls

Miniature Golf and Stuff

Miniature golf: Who'd a thunk it would still be so popular? Any day at "The Castle"—as locals know it—will find a crowd. But there's so much going on, no one spends a lot of time waiting around. There are four golf courses, all with the requisite lakes, fountains, log cabins, windmills, and waterfalls to putt through, castles, trick holes with 90-degree-angle obstacles—all the favorites. After your round, have a snack at the surprisingly varied snack bar. Chili fries, burgers, and pizza, as well as fish tacos and BLTs—and they're good! You'll want to come equipped with some serious cash, because the arcade is nonstop action. Games are flashing, bells are ringing, kids are screaming because they just won 500 tickets . . . It's damn near sensory overload. You'll find old-fashioned games like Big Bertha and Mallet Madness alongside more high-tech flash such as the Dance Revolution Fourth Mix Plus. That one has lights on a platform that light up in sequence, and as you follow along, you're dancing! And don't miss Manx Super Bike, which takes you on a dizzying course. There is so much to choose from, your best bet might be "the Special," which is a bucket of 100 tokens plus a free round of golf, all for just $20! That should

keep someone busy for a while. It's a real bargain, when you consider a round of golf alone is $5.50 for an adult and $4.50 for a
child. Add an hour or so in the arcade, and that can add up. Many
of the "skill" games spit out tickets, which can then be traded in
for goodies. For 60,000 tickets, for instance, you can get an all-in-
one stereo. For 25 tickets, you can get an alien with a parachute.
And batting cages—do they have batting cages! A nice mix of softball and baseball, with both slow-pitch and high-arc softball cages.
Baseball cages feature pitching speeds of up to 80 mph for those
who dare. It's always so heartwarming to see a dad out there in the
softball cage with his daughter, giving her pointers.

Sherman Oaks Castle Park
4989 Sepulveda Boulevard, Sherman Oaks
(818) 756-9459

Ocean Fishing and Brew-ha-ha

No matter if you are a visiting tourist or a longtime resident
of Southern California, throwing a line out in the ocean and
awaiting a strike from something unidentifiable and random, deep
from within the blue abyss, is highly addictive. It is also a bonding
experience for families, friends, and colleagues. Davey's Locker
Sportfishing in Newport Beach is the best place to go if you got
your mind on barracuda, calico bass, tuna, shark, whatever. Captain Norris will take your needs seriously and deliver the goods.
Davey's has seven charters ready to deliver you to your fish of
choice. Any of the three *Bongos* boats are available for private
chartering, while the *Western Pride* combs the coast for halibut,
sand bass, bonito, and other close-by fish. While rocking away on
the ocean waves drink a few beers (advisable only if you don't get
motion sickness!), available for purchase on any of the boats. The
Freelance is usually a three-quarter day (meaning 7 A.M.–7 P.M.)
voyage that circles the perimeter of Catalina Island. This is the
place for barracuda in spring; they practically jump into the boat.
Meanwhile, the *Pacific Star* heads out at 10 at night and returns the

following night at 5. The game? Tuna and white-bass fishing, lunkers, big fighters, trophies. Or take the *Caliber* out in pursuit of sharks. No matter what you're after, you are bound to pull in oval-eyes, blue perch, smelt, mackerel, and kelp fish, meaning you will never come home skunked. Whale-watching tours run December–March, when the whales make their migrations along the coast. And there are always a few sea lions and/or dolphins accompanying each voyage. One tip: wash your hands in lemon juice afterward, to get rid of lingering squid odors.

Davey's Locker Sportfishing
400 Main Street, Balboa
(949) 673-1434

Lost Boys Was a Fine Piece of Filmery

Pacific Park bills itself as the only amusement park on a pier. It's a treat to smell that sea air as you're whipping around the West Coaster, the roller coaster that takes you out over the ocean. And from the top of the enormous Ferris wheel, there's water as far as the eye can see. There are more sedate rides for the kids, as well as midway games such as Skee Ball and throw-the-softball-into-the-bushel-basket. Prizes to be won, bumper cars to be ridden. There's an arcade, and above the clanging and bells of games comes the unmistakable *whoosh* and *click* of AIR HOCKEY! The famous Santa Monica Pier Carousel is on the landside of the pier, and at the end of the pier is Marisol, a Mexican restaurant. Have a margarita while gazing out to sea—but it does get breezy out there. There's a food court near the middle of the pier and a fresh seafood restaurant, too, but skip them all and head to the original Hot Dog On A Stick. It's down off the pier to the south, and the fresh-squeezed lemonade and treats on a stick (hog dog, turkey, or cheese) are simply delectable. This is the place with the cute primary-color uniforms and little caps. Depending on whom you're talking to, the uniforms are either unbearably ugly or unbelievably cute and stylish. In any case, it's a dog-and-lemonade any day. The best bet at the amusement park is the Unlimited Ride Wristband, priced according to height: $8.95 for 42 inches and under, and $15.95 for everyone else. You need tickets for all the rides, and you can buy them separately if you wish. And since you're at the beach, make a day of it. Parking is conveniently located, either on the pier or right below.

Santa Monica Pier
Santa Monica
(310) 260-8744

Where a Kid Can Be a Kid

Roxbury is a great park, with two playgrounds—one for the younger set (toddlers) and one for the older crowd (ages 5–12). There's a fun dinosaur play area, with mist sprouting every few minutes, which keeps the kids screaming and guessing. The equipment is safe, after a fairly recent remodel, and there's lots of grass to run around on. It's well shaded, which is essential for the summer months. There's pretty much always an ice cream truck parked at one of the gates, and all treats are a reasonable $1.

Roxbury Park
471 S. Roxbury Drive, Beverly Hills
(310) 550-4761

Children of All Ages Enjoy the Fresh Zoysia

West Hollywood Park is another good recreational park with two play areas, one for toddlers and one for older children. It is centrally located in West Hollywood, with basketball and tennis courts and a terrific community pool. The toddlers' play area is covered during the hot summer months, and the other play area is well shaded. A tall, twirly slide is the main attraction for the older kids, but there is plenty of climbing available to all ages. You can check out balls and bats at the park office; and on the first Saturday of the month, the city hosts coffee for the parents, treats for the kids, and a moon bouncer. Free two-hour parking in the adjacent lot, and plenty of metered parking on the street.

West Hollywood Park
647 N. San Vicente Boulevard
(323) 848-6534

Make-Out Mountain

The subject of many movies is a good way to really grasp the vastness that is Los Angeles and the San Fernando Valley. The views are breathtaking, and on a clear day . . . Well, you know the rest. Start on Mulholland, just past the Hollywood Bowl, off Highland, and head west. You'll wind around the Hollywood Hills for a bit, past Runyon Canyon, past Nichols Canyon, past Laurel Canyon. Lots of unique homes, some hidden, some hanging off the hillsides. As you pass Laurel Canyon, you're heading into the serious windy road. Shortly you'll happen on Nancy Hoover Pohl Overlook at Fryman Canyon, a roomy place to stop and take in the Valley. It's also a great place to catch all the fireworks shows on that side of the hill, if you're around during Fourth of July. It does get crowded, so get there well before nine P.M., when most start. Continue on, past Bowmont, which gives you breathtaking views on both sides of the highway. A stop at Treepeople, at Coldwater Canyon and Mulholland, is a nice break. Treepeople is a Community Environmental Education Operating Center. It's lush and aromatic, and features a display called *The History of Recycling*, which is honestly quite interesting. Back out on Mulholland, after a bit, you'll have another chance to take in the scenery, at Stone Canyon Overlook. More unbelievable homes, with equally unbelievable views. Not too much longer, and you'll hit the 405, which will take you anywhere you want to go. Maybe south to the West Side and the Pier, or north, back to the Valley, or eastward to Hollywood? After this drive, you should have a much better idea of how immense and spread-out L.A. really is.

Mulholland Drive
(If you don't know, look at your Thomas Guide, for Christ's sake!)

Sunset Dinner Ride—
A Detailed Memoir

Sunset Ranch is located at the very top of Beachwood Drive, just under the Hollywood sign. It stables between sixty-five and eighty-five horses, some of them boarded, and most of them available for horseback-riding by the hour. They offer a unique way to view the city. The Sunset Ranch Friday Night Dinner Ride takes you through Griffith Park to Viva Fresh, a Mexican restaurant at the entrance to the Burbank Equestrian Center, where you tie your horse up outside before you go inside to have dinner. After dinner you're back up on the horse for the one-and-a-half-hour trip back to the stables. It leaves at six P.M. every Friday, and it's "first come, first served," so get there by five P.M. to sign up. You're back at the ranch by ten-thirty or eleven, still leaving you time for something else, if you're up for it.

One particular night, there were sixteen people in line at 4:55. It's quiet, with only the sound of horses crunching their hay, snorting, and whinnying as a soundtrack. There's a very centered German shepherd trotting among the horses, and he soon plops himself down in the middle of everything. Another dog, a herder of some sort, appears from nowhere, and positions himself between several horses. You sign a liability waiver, are offered a riding helmet, pay your money, and wait for your horse to be assigned to you.

The horses are tied up along one of the corrals. Chica, a roan horse with a gray rump, looks like a troublemaker. He's stamping at one horse who's standing too close to him, and chewing on the rope bridal of another, trying to untie it. He stays home for this ride.

It looks like a smaller group tonight. They can take up to sixty-five people, but this group will have twenty-four. There's a small group of Japanese tourists, one of them a journalist who is doing a feature on Sunset Ranch. A few date-night couples, a mother with her two teenage daughters, and several older couples round out the riders tonight. As you sign up, you indicate your level of skill: beginner, intermediate, or experienced rider. There are several riders who really know what they're doing, but for the most part, it's a beginner group. They assign horses based on your own reported skill, so if you have any experience whatsoever, it's probably safe to call yourself an intermediate. All of the horses are quite well behaved, and have been over these trails a hundred times before.

As the mounting begins, someone spots an animal on the hillside. A bobcat? We're far enough into the hills to make it plausible—but no, its tail is too long. A raccoon? No, too big. Turns out it's one of the ranch cats, and a very big one at that.

The horses are assigned: Kelly, Lucky, Sandy, Dakota, Greystone, and Cheyenne, a beautiful red-and-white pinto. Mango is given to someone with experience, and that's a good thing, as this horse definitely has a mind of his own. Ranch hands Jessica and Lucy will be guiding the group tonight, and Michael, another ranch hand, gives us the rules: Don't get off your horse. If you need help, let Jessica or Lucy know. Don't run your horse, and stay on the trails. Does everyone know his or her horse's name? That's important, because you'll have to remember it, after several margaritas at the restaurant.

We head out up the trail. Daylight savings time ended last week, and it's dark at six P.M. It doesn't take long for the city lights to come into view as you round the top of the hill. It's remarkable how bright everything is. The full moon is two days old, but with the lights of the city reflecting off the hillside, it's never pitch-black, although it is pretty dark once you get deep into the ride and don't have the view of the city from either side of the hills. There's the illuminated *Lion King* display, from the Pantages on Hollywood Boulevard, and the round Capitol Records building. The lights sparkle and shimmer, and as you head down into the

Valley you see the line of white-and-red lights on the 134, not moving. You're glad you're on a horse in the middle of Griffith Park tonight, in your own kind of gridlock.

Frogs chirp soundly, and the brush rustles with the wind. It rained just a few days ago, and the air still has that fresh sweetness that follows. The wind has the first chill of fall, and it's a good thing we've all got heavy sweaters and jackets. The ride out is a little quiet, a tad tentative, as the riders are getting used to the horses, trying to establish who's in control. "Stay no more than one horse-length behind the rider in front of you," say Jessica and Lucy, time and time again, as some riders start to really lag behind. "Squeeze with your legs, give a little kick and cluck, and he'll start trotting— let's close that gap!" One of the guides leads the way and one brings up the rear, so there's no chance of anyone getting left behind.

There are several underpasses you go through, which take you under the traffic. There's a bridge just before the restaurant that has a weight limit of six horses, so Lucy and Jessica count us off. "Don't trot, it'll make it bounce too much," they tell us as we cross the Los Angeles River. On the other side is the Longhorn Trading Post, which sells riding apparel, and looks to be set up for a neighborhood barbeque. The trail also brushes right up next to some residential areas, a lot of them horse properties.

Dismounting at Viva Fresh is another matter altogether. Riding done right is great exercise, and there's more than one pair of wobbly legs and sore seats as we hobble toward the restaurant. There are several horses tied up outside already, as Friday-night riders count this as a popular stop.

The atmosphere inside is warm and everyone is feeling good. It's Friday night, and soon you'll be saying hello to a margarita. Chips and salsa taste especially good after being on the open trail, and the margaritas do look delectable. There's one in front of almost every adult in the place, so it's obviously the thing to have. The vegetarian tostada sounds good, but doesn't exactly hit the spot. One word of advice: *Don't* pig out. As good as the Viva

Supreme Burrito ("a burrito of gargantuan proportion!") sounds—remember: you'll soon be bouncing on a horse for another hour-and-a-half jaunt.

As the country-and-western bar band swings into action, you're swinging back into the saddle again. One of the guides tells us how they used to saddle up after dinner: "Everyone find your horse, get on it, and wait for us a little way up." One can see the problems with that method. Let's start with recognizing your horse in the dark *and* after a margarita. Now the guides go through, bring each horse up, calling its name. "Who's riding Lula? Okay, left foot in the stirrup and up you go." You pass the Longhorn, and sure enough, there's about a dozen folks sitting around the table as the barbecue grills. An ice chest is filled with beer and wine bottles dot the table and it's a perfect picture of an easy Friday night.

The ride back goes much more quickly. The horses are anxious to get back; they know their work is nearly done. The Griffith Observatory peeks from between two hills, and downtown L.A. glitters just beyond that. As we come over the rise on the last hill to the stables, a pack of coyotes starts to howl from somewhere behind us up the trail. It's not scary, but wonderful and wild. It's a startling juxtaposition, with the endless lights of the busy city in front of you, and it's a little sad, because it's their home, too, but we keep taking more and more of it away from them. Civilization encroaching, right there before your very eyes.

As we arrive back at the stables, the horses all crowd over to the barn's dismounting area. Kelly the horse is standing behind Captain and rests her huge head on his equally huge rump, and it's a touching sight. These powerful animals are clearly glad the day is over. When the rider is off, the saddle, blanket, and bridle are removed and, to a horse, they gallop around for a minute, snorting and shaking their heads. They seem so happy to be free! A tip hat is put out for the guides, and everyone deposits bills into it.

Thank-yous are said all around, and as you head off down the road to the parking area, the last words you hear are, "Try not to let any of the horses out!"

Sunset Ranch also offers daily rentals every day of the week, from 9 A.M. to 5 P.M. Rates per person are $20 an hour, with a $10 deposit. Rides can be guided, if you wish. You can also schedule private dinner rides for any night except Friday, for a group of ten or more; the cost is $35 per person, not including dinner. They'll also do private lunch rides, for groups of ten or more, at $40 per person.

The dinner ride, as magical as it is, starting out in the dark, would also be quite scenic during the summer at sunset. The views from the crest of the hills can stretch to the ocean on a good day, and the sunset would be spectacular. The dinner rides go out whether there's a group of two or sixty-five, and if it's just rained, well, they'll still go. It'll just be a little muddier.

It's a most unique way not only to take in the views, but also to feel a bit of that old Wild, Wild West. It still exists, and Sunset Ranch can show you where.

Sunset Ranch
3400 Beachwood Drive, Hollywood
(323) 469-5450
www.sunsetranchhollywood.com

CHAPTER 6

Food: Eating in Los Angeles

Relative Proximity

If you have a taste for good Cajun food, but don't want to make the long trek specifically to New Orleans to get it, go to the Cajun Queen instead. Nothing like a little live jazz, provided by area legends, drifting over your garlic crawfish and étouffée, trust me. You'll see the musical notes dancing under your nose, and you'll feel like you're a million miles from Los Angeles. But, of course, you won't be that far. Situated in a Colonial-style house with an expansive park nearby, the Cajun Queen is perfect for a family outing, or for a romantic getaway where you can say to your lover, with a slow drawl, "I love you." There are creaking hardwood floors, white banisters, and a friendly waitstaff that calls you by your first name (if you tell them what it is) in an authentic Southern accent—hard to imagine for us Hollywood types. It may once have been a thriving brothel, I'm not sure. Either way, knock back a couple of Voodoo lagers in the second-story dining area, or sip some nice red wine (maybe Chianti, if you like vertigo). Everything is slower at the Cajun Queen, and indeed the pressures of city life will be exiled once you try the jambalaya and homemade French bread. Damn—the lap of luxury, right here!

Cajun Queen
1800 E. 7th Street, Charlotte, North Carolina
(704) 377-9017
(Just east of LAX)

A Dark Room for Developing Hangovers

Forget about spotting celebrities and playing it cool with models at Casa Vega in Sherman Oaks; it is pointless and absurd. Oh, they're in there all right—you just can't see them. Casa Vega is a dark, romantic restaurant with doubly potent margaritas and intestinally curious Mexican dishes. An arctic air-conditioning unit—one of the coolest in the Valley—controls the clime, just cool enough to imagine you are in Peru or Colorado, or other far-off Latin lands south of the equator. Celebrities are drawn here by magnetic pull, because, naturally, they don't want to be recognized after giving their left arms to gain fame in the first place. Casa Vega's waitstaff is benevolent enough, but ultimately they can't be bothered with petty stuff. The place is hopping all the time, and they must really concentrate to not trip over loose feet en route to delivering tequila and piping-hot combo entrées. Be kind to them. The food is dynamite, folks, and is the real reason Angelenos come here. It's as authentic as any you'll find in Los Angeles without traveling Western Avenue, and sloppy as hell. None of that "Baja-blah" and "Sharky-pooh" that has spun the ghost of Don Quixote into rotisserie.

Casa Vega
13301 Ventura Boulevard, Sherman Oaks
(818) 788-4868

The Coldstone Creamery in Sherman Oaks is an original to Los Angeles (though it has now branched into a chain), and one of the greatest ice cream parlors on earth. No fancy ice cream flavors here (like those 30-plus flavors up the road), just endless sugary ingredients to form one concoction or another. Take a look at the well-lit Wall of Fame to see what other people like, such as *"Chuck's Delight,"* a scoop or two of vanilla sweet cream, some Captain Crunch cereal pellets rolled into grain, caramel, and marshmallow, topped with rainbow sprinkles. No? Drop a suggestion and get your own recipe on the great Wall. (And don't recommend "Cookies and cream," either! That's a load of thinkless hooey, and it's oh-so-cliché.) Go for something simple, like an amaretto or peanut-butter shake. It's up to you, amateur ice cream artist. The behind-the-counter peeps will hook it up under your expert supervision. It is fun to watch them, with their metal instruments, massaging Butterfingers into base vanilla ice cream, and then squirting bottled flavor into the malleable mass. Less filling? Tastes great! And they make ice cream cakes, ice cream–cookie sandwiches, and just about anything imaginable involving your and my favorite, *ice cream*! And I tell you, the place smells like sugarplums and butternut squash, a future ice cream dish, if things go my way.

Coldstone Creamery
14622 Ventura Boulevard, Sherman Oaks (in the Lorena Plaza)
(818) 907-2702

Flaming Margaritas and Rock and Roll

Nestled right in the heart of Sunset Boulevard's Guitar Row, El Compadre is a veteran of every scene that's made its way through the local music community. It's comfortably dark, and Friday and Saturday nights find it full of hopeful scenesters on their way up the Strip. Other nights, it's long been a favorite for the denizens of the likes of Guitar Center, Freedom Guitars,

Carvin, Mesa/Boogie, and the myriad other guitar and instrument shops lining these blocks of Sunset Boulevard. Some might come for the food, reasonably priced and well portioned as it is. But most are here for the famous Flaming Margaritas. Big, icy drinks that pack a wallop, they light up the room in all sorts of ways. Half a lime, hollowed and topped with 151-proof rum, floats aflame, as the concoction is placed in front of you with a flourish. A real sight to see is a party of seven or so order these deliciously dangerous drinks—all brought out on one tray. One of these will kick-start your evening, no doubt about it. Some other rock-and-roll experiences, within a block or two: "Rock-and-Roll" Denny's, a very special place after 2 A.M. on weekends; "Rock-and-Roll" Ralph's, with plenty of shopping carts loaded only with a case of Bud and fish sticks; and the spiffed-up Sunset Grill, immortalized in song by icon Don Henley.

El Compadre
7408 W. Sunset Boulevard, Hollywood
(323) 874-7924
"Rock-and-Roll" Denny's
7373 W. Sunset Boulevard, Hollywood
(323) 876-6660
"Rock-and-Roll" Ralph's
7257 W. Sunset Boulevard, Hollywood
(323) 512-8382
Sunset Grill
7439 W. Sunset Boulevard, Hollywood
(323) 851-5557

Wine Merchant Fronting as Deli

Greenblatt's deli, right next door to the world-famous Laugh Factory, is a gold mine for the palate! As far as Jewish-style delicatessens go, they have that poetic, writer-friendly, "New York on a Sunday stroll" menu, behind observational glass, that makes the taste buds wonder. Things such as smoked whitefish and sturgeon, meat knishes, matzo ball and kreplach soups, gefilte fish, smoked tongue, corned beef or pastrami with mustard on thick rye, beet borscht, pickled green tomatoes, lox, and pickled eggs. Of course there are pastries and baked goods as well that make the face sweat just imagining their decadence. All of these items are delicious, and somehow endearing to the eater—let us make no mistake. Even the aromas of this deli bring to mind the feeling of big-city vastness. But what distinguishes Greenblatt's from common delicatessens like Jerry's is the wine shop! Greenblatt's is an expert in imported wines and liqueurs, as well as domestic stuff. There is something for everybody, every budget, every bouquet, every tolerance level. Cabernet, merlot, sauvignon blanc, chardonnay, Chianti, pinot, zinfandel, Bordeaux, white, red, redwood- or steel-distilled—you name it, they got it. They are on the point system, and range in price widely depending on your appreciation of the product. And Greenblatt's has exotic tequilas, rums, vodkas in ultrastylish bottles with long Scandinavian necks, bourbons, and cognacs and brandies (which are the same thing, if you ask me). Louis XIV would be overcome with tears at the sight of it. What astonishing regality!

Greenblatt's
8017 Sunset Boulevard, Hollywood
(323) 656-0606

When in Rome, Try the Argentinean Food

Every time Ma and Pa come to town, inevitably we end up at the Gaucho Grill. They don't have many—if any—Argentinean restaurants back home in Michigan, after all; but here in Los Angeles, we have our fair share of this kind of cuisine, a good and unexpectedly light blend of mostly unadulterated (or lightly seasoned) meat dishes (you got your chicken, you got your steak . . .) with a great selection of sides (you got your fresh salad, you got your fries, you got the best damn mashed potatoes anywhere).

Though not necessarily the last word on Argentinean food, the Gaucho chain, with satellites in L.A., the Valley, and on the Third Street Promenade in Santa Monica, is a great and well-priced "starter kit" of sorts. Their empanadas (deep-fried cheese or vegetable pockets) are a key appetizer, and the Milanese (a battered and lightly fried thin steak) is simply delicious; the Manager's Special salad—a vaguely spicy Gaucho Grill original—is an excellent choice, as well. But by the time you've downed all the free bread dipped in their awesome chimichurri sauce (a secret mixture of oil, parsley, lemon, and a lot of South American magic), you might not even be able to completely finish your meal. Beware, the Argentine folk do feed their guests very, very well. Oh—and for the most part, vegans need not apply.

Gaucho Grill on Sunset
7980 W. Sunset Boulevard, Los Angeles
(323) 656-4152
Gaucho Grill at the Beverly Center
121 La Cienega Boulevard, Beverly Hills
(310) 657-9104

Doff to The Hat

So you have an appetite and are looking for something hearty to stick on your bones because you have been called ultraskinny and frail, and that really hurts, of course, so the reasonable thing to do, the smart thing to do, is to go to The Hat, which claims to have "world-famous pastrami," and they are right, because it is the world's *best* pastrami, too, and it is lean, with mustard and pickles and all kinds of nutritional secrets that are bound to add girth and pleasure to your somber being regardless of your heritage, so much so that when you order a large fries or onion rings, you are given a "grocery bag" of them, which causes one to think, *Wow, that sure is a lot of food*, but then it dawns on you—"*I have leftovers for tomorrow*"—and anybody who is anybody knows pastrami and onion rings are better on Day Two, as are wet fries with gravy and other sandwiches of all sorts—all of them hearty, so hearty that ain't nobody gonna call you "skinny-ass" anymore, because you will have world-famous pastrami in your bodyworks that melts like butter on the palate and sticks like adhesive to your torso and eventually has you saluting and winking at the fifty-year-old and legendary Hat. It's good.

The Hat
Alhambra: Garfield and Valley
Brea: Imperial and State College
Glendora: Route 66 and Grand
Monterey Park (the original): Atlantic and Riggin
Pasadena: Lake and Villa
Simi Valley: Los Angeles and Williams
Temple City: Rosemean and Broadway
Upland: 11th and Central

The Resemblance Is . . . Not Exactly Perfect

If I didn't know that Elvis would be 67 if he was alive now, I'd say he wasn't dead, and that I'd been privy to one of those rare sightings reserved for the King himself and other rock secondary gods such as Jim "Lizard King" Morrison. If it was at all linearly possible, I might then go on to say that Elvis has been reincarnated. But, judging from the lines on the well-tanned face of the guy they affectionately call Thai Elvis around that part of Hollywood now known as Thai Town, one can easily surmise that this man spent at least part of his life living on earth at the same time his idol did. Still, the likeness is nearly uncanny. From the oversized shades to the purple cape, to the giant, studded belt to the platform heels on his feet, this guy has, as they said about Elvis, more soul than he can possibly control. He moves. He grooves. He raises his hands in the air. He sings the hits and more with . . . a slight accent. Still, any way you slice it, this "Elvis" show at Palms Thai Restaurant (begins at 7:30 every night except Monday) is a real hoot. And the food and service (one night, we literally had three waitresses check up on us in a span of five minutes) are darn good, too. Check it out some time when you're hungry and hungry for a hunk of burning love.

Palms Thai Restaurant
5273 Hollywood Boulevard, Los Angeles
(323) 462-5073

Venice in the Morning Is Nice, Right?

Locals know all about the House of Teriyaki, Too, aka the Hot House. Just a block from the salty ocean waters sits this peaceful neighborhood hangout, almost in perfect harmony with the lifestyles indigenous to Venice Beach. A few stragglers from the tourist-friendly boardwalk make their way over to Hot, but mostly this is a local place, where people come with their dogs, their skateboards, their Rastafarian duds, their deck of tarot cards, and their flip-flops. Bohemia has found a home right here at Hot. The breakfast and lunch menu is fairly basic—except that they have ostrich burgers—and completely affordable. The highest price on the entire menu is $6.49, but mostly everything costs between $3.99 and $4.99. The banana pancakes are great, as are the omelets and the fresh-squeezed orange juice. But the coffee is phenomenal, fresh-roasted and lingeringly tasty (and the creamer is thick!). There is a patio for outdoor seating, and bench tables indoors, in promotion of community. Most notably, there are always smiles at Hot. Now open for dinner.

House of Teriyaki, Too
1715 Pacific Avenue, Venice
(310) 396-9938

West Coast Cholesterol Is Better than Midwestern

Once a pure southern California play, In-n-Out Burgers is the Holy Grail for a lot of burger lovers. "Nothing frozen," they say, and you can taste it. No heat lamps, freezers, or microwaves allowed. Hand-leafed lettuce, french fries that were actual pota-toes not too long ago, real ice cream milkshakes—it's another one of those, "As soon as we get to L.A., I've got to have a Double Double." For the uninitiated, that's two patties and two slices of cheese. You can have any number of patties and slices of cheese, and the "4 by 4" is another popular size with the good eaters. Everything is completely fresh, made-to-order, and mouthwatering. The drive-through can get crowded late at night and at lunch, but inside, they keep things moving. The menu is simple: burgers, cheeseburgers, fries, milkshakes, and beverages. Started by Harry and Esther in Baldwin Park in 1948, In-n-Out has grown to 140 locations today, encompassing Nevada and Arizona. Family-owned since the beginning, it's famous for treating employees like family, with good starting wages and benefits.

In-n-Out Burgers
Select locations:
Hollywood: 7079 Sunset Boulevard
Studio City: 3640 Cahuenga Boulevard
Burbank: 761 N. San Fernando Road
West L.A.: 9215 W. Venice Boulevard
North Hollywood: 5864 Lankershim Boulevard
www.in-n-out.com

So What About the Germans?

Pass by the stone lions, enter through the heavy wooden door, and prepare to be transported to the Prussian Empire, for inside this kooky palace are beer steins aplenty as well as a goodly amount of suits of armor, wooden casks, elaborate chandeliers and endless stone arches; heck, there are even stuffed moose and deer heads and relief's showing holy men and knights adorning the walls of this wonderful German eatery. Lowenbrau Keller borders Koreatown, but certainly has more the feel of some eccentric Bavarian tourist trap (it's hard to ignore the travel posters featuring a lederhosen-clad man and his smiling frau). The food, meanwhile, is pure German woodsman: meat, meat, and more meat (and good German beer, too!); and there is delicious schnitzel, smoked pork, sausage, and steak served in hearty portions. On the side, come two types of kraut, golden fried potatoes, and giant steamed carrots. With smiling, sometimes stern, waitresses, sporting real German accents and wishing you "good evening, children," Lowenbrau Keller must make the country descended from the Teutonic race proud.

Lowenbrau Keller
3211 Beverly Boulevard, Los Angeles
(213) 382-5723

And Let's Not Forget the Red Lion

The sign on the upstairs patio, says "Berlin, Germany" thataway, which actually means that right here, on this spot, you can eat, drink, and smoke it up nightly in this festive little Octoberfest near the heart of Silver Lake. After devouring my delicious chicken schnitzel and downing a couple of Hefeweizen, I walked toward a small hallway in the back, before the waitress, wearing a traditional dress and flowers behind her ear, stopped me and said no, that's the owner's apartment: "the little man's room is over there." Yes, this place is full of little nooks and crannies: a bar on the main floor; another, like a hidden grotto, in a tiny room at the top of the stairs; and then, of course, the aforementioned patio, where umbrellas protect one from the rays of the sun and umlauted words on woodcut signs advertise all kinds of brauts, dogs, and libations. Beer three and I was ready to throw it all up in the air and spend the night bopping from room to room, possibly even playing up the European thing to the fullest by walking arm in arm with my buddy, from tabletop to tabletop; from drinking song to drinking song; from—hell, why not—frau to frau. Signs be damned, this is Germany. And I'm fricking on vacation! As the patio filled to capacity and various L.A.-ites began to cheer on the Lakers playing on Red Lion's giant TV screen, I began to hum a little tune to myself: "Mann kann nicht zu fiel Bier trinken." Yes, one cannot drink enough beer (or have too much fun, for that matter) in this little side of Berlin known as Red Lion.

Red Lion Tavern
2366 Glendale Boulevard, Silver Lake
(323) 662-5337

"I Love Her Very Much"

Belly dancing is a cultural wonder to a dumb American like me, and I tell you . . . it feels uncomfortable thinking of it in mere terms of arousal. Surely that would be trespassing on sacred ground, methinks. At least, it seems to contain the mystery of a ritualistic sacrament, right? Go to Mamounia. It will show you just how culturally deficient you (and I) are. You may not solve the mystery that is belly dancing, but you *will* see it up close in an authentic Moroccan-restaurant atmosphere. The place is dark and intimate, with covered lanterns to prevent the swirling belly dancers from setting the place afire. There is no menu, no expectations, no negative vibes. It *is* pure decadence, though. The *bastilla*, a pastry appetizer with ground chicken, almonds, and egg in the piping hot middle, is delightful to eat with your fingers. You will feel nine years old again. Everything is veiled in intrigue, from the knee-high hassocks to the white *gambazes* the waiters wear. The large fruit basket/boat is overwhelming, with grapes the size of plums, accompanied by baklava and fresh mint tea. Then the music gets louder, and the lights grow dimmer, and the dervish with finger cymbals comes out and entrances her content onlookers. That's when the red wine, or the Casablanca ale, starts to feed unfamiliar impulses into your brain and the next thing you know, you are stuffing a dollar into her underthings. For such opulent ambience, the place is considerably festive and lighthearted. A great experience.

Mamounia
132 N. Robertson Boulevard, Beverly Hills
(310) 360-7535

Bottled Milk in Los Angeles?

Not everything is leaning toward futurism, damn it. There is still the fight of the traditionalists, grounding our timeless Rockwell idyll against the onrushing current of machines! To hell with Los Angeles, the "pioneer"! Introducing Los Angeles the "conservative!" At Broguiere's fresh farm dairy in Montebello (aka the Montebello Sanitary Dairy), the nostalgic feeling of the drive-in dairy farm is intact. Cars can drive right up to the checkstand and place their orders for fresh eggs, bottled Broguiere's milk, ice cream, cheese, butter, and other fresh products. The motto is "Milk So Fresh . . . the Cow Doesn't Know It's Missing." That's funny. And true. Broguiere's seasonal eggnog is as good as it gets, and perfect for that brandy drink you've been contemplating having by the December fireplace. Wear your green woolen sweater with the big snowflake; it brings out your eyes. And sip that eggnog! It is thick, creamy, and utterly off-the-charts in cholesterol content, which is okay because it is a treat, a "once in a while" thing. The chocolate milk is not far behind the eggnog and will become a regular addictive substance for those who are willing. An old milk wagon parked out front announces your arrival. The place has been around since 1920! Bring your bottles for a dollar back on quart-sized bottles and a buck-fifty on the half-gallon. And forget about grocery-store plastics! Milk tastes better out of a bottle.

Montebello Sanitary Dairy/Broguiere's
505 S. Maple Avenue, Montebello
(323) 726-0524

Seafood and Ocean Mist

Enjoy a nice seaside meal with fresh seafood and a leisurely deck from which to gaze out onto the ocean? Like the stentorian revving of multiple Harley-Davidsons roaring in unison? Check it out: Neptune's Net in Malibu. Featured in such noteworthy films as *The Fast and the Furious*, Neptune's Net is hardly suckered into a singular theme. Bikers love it, as do families with tykes, albino people, and families without tykes. There is a gift shop, a fresh-catch seafood counter to order up crab, lobster, oysters, and shrimp, and a separate counter for ordering fish and chips, hamburgers, hot dogs, and the like. And the greatest aspect of Neptune's is that it is right across the street from prime beach-plots to lay your weary, alabaster torso out in the sun. If you're a visiting tourist, go for no other reason than to experience the dichotomy that exists between bikers and their insistence on living every day as if they were back in Sturgis, South Dakota. If you live in Los Angeles, go to remind yourself that it is okay to go a couple of days without showering and to keep your lazy gut. And go, of course, for the fresh shrimp!

Neptune's Net
44505 Pacific Coast Highway, Malibu
(310) 457-3095

Like Coming Home

Despite its *très* L.A. clientele North somehow seems like home to me. Sure, the bartenders in my house would be quicker, and guests would without a doubt be required to check all cell phones at the door. And I suppose there'd probably be clothes strewn all over the floor if North were my place. But then, it's not; and so the place is rather tidy and quite cozy. The comforting, flatteringly lit wood-grain entrance space at North leads one by staircase down into the pit of the building, where the calming, pale, underlit bar and plenty of plush booths await all the pretty people who come here. DJs play good and funky, though a little too loud, music of the hip-hop and dance variety. And the food, a nice selection of California cuisine, is tasty . . . and much better than the stuff I make at my run-down apartment.

North
8029 Sunset Boulevard, Los Angeles
(323) 654-1313

Now, That's a Spicy-a Meatball, Eh?

This is the granddaddy of all places to bring the family. Service is quick, the food is inexpensive and good, the bread is endless, applesauce comes with the kids' meals, and they have crayons. There's nothing over $9.25 on the menu, and all dinners include salad, beverage (coffee, tea, or milk), and ice cream for dessert. I'd suggest the Manager's Special for the grown-ups—and make it the combination of marinara sauce and mizithra cheese. You can even upsize the portion for an extra $1.50, for those exceptionally good eaters, and there's a full bar to boot. The kids' meals are real deals. For $3.50 you'll get your choice of, among other things, spaghetti, with or without meatballs, or macaroni and cheese; applesauce or salad, a drink, and ice cream. It can get really crowded at night, especially on the weekends, and even for large parties there are no reservations. But don't let that deter you, as they manage to move everybody through unbelievably quickly, but not so you feel rushed at the table. It's an immense place, with many antique-filled rooms, so there's lots of room. A few video games in the bar can keep the kids occupied for the wait, as well.

The Old Spaghetti Factory
5939 W. Sunset Boulevard, Los Angeles
(323) 469-7149

An Unexplainable Phenomenon
Crop circles, Stonehenge, Area 51 (or Studio 54, for that matter)—these have nothing on Pink's, which, seen from a car after the obligatory L.A. two A.M. bar closing time (or just about any other time), seems more a Meccalike religious experience than a mere hot dog stand. For people come from miles around L.A. just to stand in a fluorescent-lit line for a good half-hour (sometimes more) in the wee morning hours (and at the precious lunchtime crunch)—and all for what? A greasy hamburger? Some thick chili fries? A dog with everything? There has to be more to it than that. Yet some of today's greatest minds (for example, my friend, Stan Bolinowitz, an actor and veterinarian by trade, said when asked: "I just don't get it") are still hard-pressed to explain it. Some have conjectured that it has something to do with the

moon's gravitational pull (the full moon itself was ruled out when it was shown that even during a crescent period, the hordes still come), the astrological chart, and an arcane text called the *Zagat's* guide. But no solid proof has been published as of yet. Regardless, if your stay in L.A. lasts more than a few days, you, too, may feel a strong desire to stop and enjoy a nice tub of onion rings or a chili dog with everything at Pink's.

Pink's Hot Dogs
711 N. La Brea Avenue, Los Angeles
(323) 931-4223

"Time to Make the Donuts!" (Our Temple)
One of the highly visible declarations of Los Angeles' independence stands brazenly in the smoggy air of Inglewood, under a daily fresh coat of pigeon icing. It is the great golden donut that designates Randy's Donuts, a beautifully constructed cartoonlike edifice that has had policemen of that jurisdiction folding over in cardiac arrest for nearly fifty years (designed by Robert Graham, and open since 1953). Forget about Bob's Big Boy, big boy, this place is keener. All the baked goods are fresh at Randy's, and delicious. And guess what, you anorexic women with silicone chests: If you act now there will be no calories in the donuts, no fat, no sugar, no sodium. They'll be 100 percent organic. Eat as many as you like. Discontinue reading here if you are one of these anorexic women. Gone? Good. (Here's the thing, folks. These donuts are loaded with all the goodness of any other donut shop, and even more fat than usual. It is essential that anorexic women eat with a clear conscious, though, so we lie. But I digress.) Randy's specializes in jelly donuts, chocolate, cream-filled, plain cake, and with sprinkles, as well as long johns, bear claws, and twists. And probably a lot more, for that matter.

Randy's Donuts
805 W. Manchester Avenue, Inglewood
(310) 645-4707

Bock, Bock, Bock . . . Thank You, Easter Bunny?

If you are visiting Los Angeles and want to experience something incomprehensibly delightful, and your heart can afford some well-conceived cholesterol levels, then Roscoe's House of Chicken and Waffles is a must. The twenty-five-year-old establishment is a favorite among locals, for the homemade waffles and succulent chicken, as well as mouthwatering vittles that would have Aunt Bess back there in Mississippi peeing her pants with excitement. Strangely enough, the combination of waffles and chicken is excellent. But that's only the half of it: there are collard greens, giblets, livers, red beans and rice, grits, egg dishes, and sweet-potato pie (the real deal) to enjoy. Lots of celebrity types eat here, including the late rapper, the Notorious B.I.G., who was always "flossing ho's at Roscoe's," you see, and indeed, a great number of girls with shapely figures are right here. Not only is the food down-home delicious, but there is some great merchandise for sale to prove you were there. (Statistics have proven you will look smart to your friends back home when they see you wearing a Roscoe's T-shirt.) Be patient, as there is usually a line, but the wait is worth it.

The Original Roscoe's House of Chicken and Waffles
1514 N. Gower Street (at Sunset), Hollywood
(323) 466-7453 or (323) 466-9329

Heard It Through the Grapevine . . .

Interestingly enough, the San Antonio Winery survived Prohibition days by serving "sacramental wine" until the law slackened in 1933. It is now the only pre-Prohibition winery in Los Angeles. In fact, it is the *only* winery in Los Angeles; the last of over one hundred that once lined the Los Angeles River Basin, back when downtown had a Little Italy. Today it is a historic monument that has been renovated quite nicely to preserve its nostalgic feel. The San Antonio Winery offers tours through the premises, where spectators can learn the process of fermentation, which wines are regulated by temperature, what differentiates a dry wine from a sweet wine, and the difference between redwood barrels and stainless-steel barrels. An astounding capacity of 1.5 million gallons of wine is stored, made, and bottled here. There is also an elegant restaurant serving large-portioned pasta dishes, and a wine counter to sample the multitude of vinos the shop exports. The family-owned operation has an air of significance and is ultimately inspiring, regardless of your wine palate. Here's wassailing Santa Cambianica, the original founder, who skirted the lean days of Prohibition! Open seven days.

San Antonio Winery
737 Lamar Street, Downtown
(323) 223-1401

A Cuban Dream

This Cuban-cuisine dream of a local chain is good and cheap and, surprisingly, still pretty classy—the perfect place to take an unsuspecting date, in other words. Or just get drunk with pals on hefty pitchers of sangria, or bottled beers with Latino flair and the bonus of a lemon wedge. I, a notorious menu procrastinator, usually end up getting the garlic chicken–and–onions dish with a side of black beans, rice, and—best of all—Versailles' trademark battered and fried plantains. But there are plenty of other good things to choose from, including paella and a vast meat and seafood selection, making Versailles both an awesome beginning to a larger evening, or just a great and energetic weekday dinner spot.

Versailles
10319 Venice Boulevard, Culver City
(310) 558-3168
Also:
1415 S. La Cienega Boulevard, Los Angeles
(310) 289-0392

Best Cure for a Hangover

Damn it all. As you're reeling from the hangover from last night, your pal is reading from his travel guide and gaily pointing out the

RESIDENT TOURIST: LOS ANGELES

sign for The World Café on Hollywood Boulevard, saying something like: "This place has some of L.A.'s best all-night clubs, such as Club Bang and Beat It. We should go here tonight." *Tonight?* you think. *If I don't get something greasy in my stomach right now, I'm going to puke and then fall asleep forever.* Too bad the travel tome your buddy holds doesn't say something about The World Café's restaurant. As you turn green on this warm Saturday, you walk past the building's glass door not knowing your cure was so close at hand. Yes, while the rest of the club kids are gently sleeping off their "E" buzzes from the night before at The Ruby, The World Café (or El Mundo, as it is also known) is, unbeknownst to even most L.A. residents, serving up a wonderful cure for the head- and body aches commonly associated with alcohol consumption—that is, Peruvian food. It took us, too, some time to find out that these South American types know how to make such a panacea. Also, we didn't know that they had french fries down there. Even if they don't, really, it's cool with us. For our money (and next-day stomach-acid problems), we'll take The World Café's brilliant mixture of greasy onions, tomatoes, fries, and choice of chicken or steak (called *Saltado de Pollo* and *Lomo Saltado*, respectively), down it with a big, fat Coke, and watch as your pains drift away and turn into delectable fat. By the end of it all, had you known to come here, you'd certainly be saying: "Yeah, maybe I'll put on my fishnet stockings and vampire teeth and we'll go to club Clockwork Orange here tonight."

The World Café at The Ruby
7070 Hollywood Boulevard, Los Angeles
(323) 467-7070

The Most Important Meal, from Frills to None

As expected, even breakfast in L.A. can have a decidedly überhip quality to it if you go to the right (or wrong, depending on your own trendy tendencies) place. The Griddle Café, near the Directors Guild building, is a high-maintenance affair, complete with various expensive fruit-topped cakes and pretty industry types fretting over last night's drunken affairs. Swingers has a slightly more down-to-earth appeal, although don't let the cool jukebox suck you in too far. You'll still end up paying dearly for a tofu omelet among rock-dream folks who have purposely tousled their hair and put on their best leather (if they're not already still wearing it from the night before) for the occasion. Up the street a bit, the Kings Road Café is a decadent, preppy little place where you'll eat your pesto eggs amid sporty (notice all the striped jogging pants) out-of-work actors who will be considering how they'll pay for their meal. A step down from these, and *positively* more down-to-earth, is the grungy but fun Duke's on Sunset, which used to be on Santa Monica Boulevard. Incidentally, Jim Morrison is reputed to have gone to the old location every morning to start a day that would no doubt last until a late breakfast the next day (and repeat). Had Jim Morrison known about it, however, he probably would have gone to our favorite, Ye Rustic Café on Hillhurst Avenue, where on weekends from ten A.M. to one P.M. you can watch the game and get a great breakfast (a few combos to choose from) and a drink (yes, that includes the alcoholic kind; of special note is the bloody Mary) for only five buckaroonies. We, too, never went for the idea that a healthy breakfast alone will cure a hangover.

The Griddle Café
7916 W. Sunset Boulevard, Los Angeles
Swingers
8020 Beverly Boulevard, Los Angeles
Kings Road Café
8361 Beverly Boulevard, Los Angeles
Duke's
8909 Sunset Boulevard, West Hollywood
(310) 652-3100
Ye Rustic Café
1831 Hillhurst Avenue, Los Angeles
(323) 666-3524

Ring around the Rosy Ice Cream

In twenty-three years, brothers Mashti and Matt Scivani have blossomed into *the* ice-cream makers of Los Angeles. How? By using the ingredients of Mother Earth. Rosewater ice cream. Saffron-pistachio ice cream. Ginger and cardamom and orange blossom ice creams. Every bit as delectable and tantalizing as their names. They are spin-offs of traditional Persian favorites, but who knew that America would flip over tasting the flavors of flowers like this? The two owners of Mashti Malone's Ice Cream, that's who. Located next door to the Lava Lounge, Mashti is not exactly famous *yet*, but the word-of-mouth praise is spreading locally, regionally, nationally (especially now that they ship their ice cream to faraway places). If you stop in only once, try the original flavor of plain rosewater ice cream perhaps as a sandwich between two light wafers. Or try the rosewater ice (aka rose sorbet), a complex carbohydrate that looks like frozen glass noodles and is best when accompanied by lemon juice or sour cherry syrup. Amazing stuff, truly. And healthier than the regular ice cream. Lactose-intolerant? No worry, much of the ice cream is dairy-free. If you go often, try each and every one of the flavors to grasp the whole beautiful range of goodness. Mashti Malone's has a couple of cool quirks, too. It provides dry ice to a large number of studios in the Holly-wood area and is a great place to get it for your Halloween party. They also supply more than 200 restaurants in southern California. All by distilling a few roses and making something utterly heavenly and edible! For those of you looking for an alternative Mother's Day or Valentine's Day gift, call Mashti Malone's and have them ship it to your loved one's door. Beats hell out of carnations!

Mashti Malone's Ice Cream
1523 N. La Brea Avenue, Hollywood
(323) 874-0144 or toll-free (866) ROSEICE

CHAPTER 7

Museums and Art in Los Angeles

The North Hollywood Arts District

Famous evangelist/conquistador/actor Stan Bolinowitz and I recently met at a charming café in North Hollywood, and discussed a range of interesting topics over a fresh strudel and several cups of dark coffee. It was memorable, though when I think back, it seems the conversation never took place at all. Stan is like a ghost who carries his well-manicured flesh like a heavy burden. He is stratospheric, as many of you in the public eye already know, he sees all, from the rooftops of humanly elevation. Being the terse, coyote-chasing linguist that he is, Stan spoke to me mostly through his eyes—those unblinking mirrors of infinity that are slightly jaundiced and wildly radical. I saw the wholesomeness of a saint in those eyes. He also spoke to me verbally, but only upon my insistence—alas, the handheld tape recorder wasn't picking up the astral dialogue. I asked him directly what he thought of

North Hollywood, and if he felt it was a real "arts district." This was a question of mild interest to me at first, to fish out some of his wisdom, but it turned into a cathartic revelation that I was fortunate enough to get on tape. This had me wanting to trace the steps of his apotheosis to its origins, but I wouldn't dare trespass like that! His words had me paralyzed by their stunning precision, all centered on the twenty-year-old arts district where we dined. Following is a transcript of his response, relayed to me in that Southern drawl that made him famous in 1974, in his role as Van Nordan in *Cheap Leather Suit*. Dear reader, I present Stan Bolinowitz's idea of North Hollywood:

"The North Hollywood Arts District," he said, "is an immune system trying to overcome the egocentric toxins reproducing all around it. One merely needs to look at the movie studios and the academy buildings [the Academy of Television Arts and Sciences] that lie upon this infant art world like a pox. NoHo is mining for artistic sincerity on the icy surface of infertile glacial plains, to put it more indirectly. That is frustrating. A real humdingy effort [*sic*]. Typical to the Los Angeles community, North Hollywood has a few fanatics who constitute the bulk of personality here, and who act as ambassadors to the scene. And then a couple thousand vague supporters, mostly residents and local newspapers, and an indeterminable number of loose egos that want to know what it—the NoHo Arts District, as it is thoughtfully coined—can do for them, should they get involved. NoHo has all kinds of painters, musicians, pediatricians, poets, morticians, harlequins, carnival folk, teetotalers, lemurs, and esoteric shop-owners, not to mention great restaurants and theaters and galleries and murals. My favorite sushi joint is Tokyo Delves, because I always receive the warmest ovation when I come in. And the yellowfin is aggressive on the morning slide, which is always appreciated at my age. A couple of those and . . . *plop* . . . *plop*. . . ."

Here he paused to reflect on something, an eerie silence that lasted upward of a minute, and produced a gratuitous smile that stretched his famous Rollie Fingers mustache three inches off his face. Then he resumed:

"But if you ask me is it a real arts district, I say no, not really. Los Angeles in general has no sense of community; too much vanity, not enough altruism for a support system, no brother-hood, no feeling of intimacy. Besides, the people are too fat. Take the Chelsea scene in New York City. In its day the largest of the artists weighed 120 pounds. The average NoHo artist is well over that. And I mean *well* over that. Girth is the primary problem with North Hollywood. They must narrow the belt line to make it more artsy. Plus, didn't I just say that pediatri-cians comprise some of the art scene? Come on! How does that translate into art?"

After a quick exchange of shrugged shoulders he took a breath, and gave me what I wanted. A fire-dialed prolixity that tinted the afternoon with the most profound shades of gray.

"You're not happy, Chuck? You want me to break down the beauty of North Hollywood for you? To laud the seers and the pioneers, and stamp my feet to Willie Nelson's 'On the Road Again'?" (He deduces from my nervous shift that consent has been granted to continue.) "All right, I will. Just between the two of us, NoHo has potential, because vanity and self-acceptance are married here. People are content with themselves, enough to make progress, and they are vain enough to follow their vision through. Look at the galleries of artwork, and the bohemian coffeehouses like Eagles, and the street fairs with psychic jugglers, loud bands with helmets, flying stuffed animals, sidewalk fashion shows, the storefronts, all of that; look at these things as a portent. This place has many artistic seeds planted in the right places that are just now taking bloom, enough to potentially overtake the longstanding corporate rule, if you like metaphorisms [sic]. The cancers here are mercenary, but they are being purged. You get what I'm saying, Chuck? Wipe your face, you have some strudel dangling from your chin. . . ."

"Now listen, there are several notable members of the NoHo board of directors who have the gonads to make something happen. David Dion, the owner of that shop with the pimp gear and vinyl suits, Vavoom! on Lankershim, has gotten himself arrested for painting a sidewalk! It wasn't graffiti or anything, hell no—it was actual artwork. And it was only a stretch of sidewalk, known as 'the porch' to all the businesses on that strip, in front of his store and consensual neighboring stores, kind of an ecclesiastical theme that was actually quite nice. Well, the city came down on him with regulation balderdash. Slapped his ass red. Said something about toxicity, and spat on his idea of degentrification. He is rightfully piqued, understand? But he continues to provoke change in the name of this art scene. And hey, the man makes the sexiest women's undergarments in the land, and can't be bothered with laws. To him, I lift my Colombian roast."

(While his coffee cup is lifted, I see that peculiarly greenish vein on his forehead showing through the skin.)

"I see you like that, Chuck. Your gestures are transparent. Take Carlos Vera, who owns the Our Story art gallery, a regular savior here, and one of the stalwarts who's in for the long haul. Or Peter Strauss over at the Raven Playhouse, a visionary as I understand the word. He is a man devoted to the theater arts, who understands the selflessness involved in creation. These are the martyrs of the NoHo arts scene. You see that dojo over there? Look familiar? It was the Cobra Kai in *The Karate Kid*. Take a closer look, Chuck. Fear *does* exist in that dojo, doesn't it? Plus, I may not be an expert in geology [*sic*], but this isn't Reseda. Art? Come on! And don't get me started about Carl Crew of the California Institute of Abnormal Arts! Here is a man, a former mortician, who shakes your hand and the blood runs cold, who harbors circus-sideshow freaks in his domain as if they were monks, who boasts of his mummified clown on display as a delicacy for our senses. Carl is a character from Kafka's brilliantly demented mind. Or how about his ancient fairy from Scotland, which he will explain, in all seriousness, is a kind of amulet; or the severed arm of St. Claude de Lorraine in a glass display case with candlelight vigils—does that sound like art? CIA has Iggy Pop and general freak videos, along with that cult classic *Pink Flamingos* on a loop, dear sir. Everything contains art in this sanctuary of carnie life. Carl affectionately refers to the NoHo Arts District as the 'so-so arts district,' because that is his way of recruiting madness to join him. He loves bearded children, too, which is something we share in common. I have always been partial to premature facial hair. You like bearded children, Chuck?"

"Yes. But what about . . ."

"I have enlightened you enough, dear straggler. End of interview."

With that, the brilliant Stan Bolinowitz rose from the table and left. I finished what was remaining of his strudel, drank the cold dregs of his dark coffee, and reflected on what he had told me. I thought to myself: *What a wonderful world.* Just kidding. I really thought to myself: *Stan's lips were just on this cup.* Talk about my heart going a-flutter! Mostly I wondered if what I just heard was real. I mean, that perfection of logic that rolled off his tongue so effortlessly; that magnetic stare that burned through my irises so cleanly as to leave me seared; the way his voice guided over the topic en route to a subconscious summary—golly, the man *emancipated* me. Whether his notions of NoHo are right or wrong (they were right), I sure felt artistic just then. And you know what, reader? The air is gravid with art in NoHo, regardless how immature the scene is. Go for yourself. And if you're lucky, maybe you will see the great Stan Bolinowitz doing something brilliant, like I did.

Vavoom!
5221 Lankershim Boulevard, North Hollywood
(818) 769-8700
Raven Playhouse
5233 Lankershim Boulevard, North Hollywood
(818) 509-9519

CIA (California Institute of Abnormal Arts)
11334 Burbank Boulevard, North Hollywood
(818) 506-6353

L.A. Radio

You would think that in the music-industry capital of the world,
where the car is the most-used form of transportation, it'd be easy
to find good radio. For the most part, L.A.'s radio is just as flat and
boring as the rest of the nation's. At the end of the day, even the
city's supposed "alternative rock" station, KROQ, comes off as an
evil ratings-mad behemoth which overplays to death any catchy
tune it gets its hands on. The more watered-down (read:"less
heavy") format comes with Star 98.7, which features smarmy DJ
and local celebrity Ryan Seacrest, who is as handsomely glib as
they come. Still, if '80s music is your thing, the following do offer
decent retro shows: KROQ's *Flashback Lunch* (noon to one P.M.
weekdays) features the exaggerated English accent of Richard
Blades; and Star's Totally '80s at noon (you want '60s and '70s,
folks, just try the classic-rock stations at 93.1 or 95.5 FM). On the
weekends, KROQ features a late-night show on Sundays at midnight, hosted by Rodney Bingenheimer, a local personality who
was, in the 1970s, a premier promoter and man-about-town with
his fab club, Rodney's English Disco (which has, incidentally, been
resurrected at Tempest on Tuesday nights). With his Rodney on
the ROQ, Bingenheimer continues to showcase the most cutting-
edge stuff from the UK and beyond, in his own decidedly not-DJ
way. KBIG 104.3 plays pretty lame straight pop, but it, too, has a
good "blast from the past" show, KBIG Disco Saturday Night (6
P.M.–3 A.M.), which is a favorite among the young and drunk-
and-driving.

As for sounds on the cutting edge, there's not a lot; however,
KCRW is the station of choice for the shabby chic. Run out of

Santa Monica college, its playlist is avant-garde, though in a "white," somewhat pretentious way. On Sundays from eleven to two A.M. this station—located at 89.9 on the dial—goes all-out weird and interesting with a show by Joe Frank, who apparently enjoys tape-recording the conversations about life he has with his friends, or waxing philosophical—dark music playing in the background—about his failed relationships with baggage-ridden women. On the other hand, KXLU (88.9 FM), a community service of Loyale Marymount college, offers a great but rough smattering of even edgier music; that is, if you can get it to come in.

As for news, KCRW has a great "local-angle" commentator, Warren Olney, on weekdays from six-thirty to seven P.M. While in the AM frequencies, you've got a few information sources to choose from, but KFWB (980 AM) seems to stand out as a reliable start. KFI, for its part, is more appreciated for its weekday lineups, including John and Ken (3 P.M.–7 P.M.), who do a good (though generally conservative) tag-team job of filtering perspective out of current events; a few hours (7 P.M.–10 P.M.) from the brilliant absurdist Phil Hendrie; and later (10 P.M.–5 A.M.), from everybody's favorite conspiracy theorist, Art Bell. KABC (790 AM), meanwhile, has a good show in *Mr. KABC* (10 P.M.–1 A.M.), as he tries to answer (or get his callers to answer) all your obscure questions. The "all-talk" FM station 97.1 is a safe bet for those tired of looking for music, too, as they have Howard in the mornings and at night Conway and Steckler (8 P.M.–11 P.M.), a couple of local smart-alecks who have their "current topic" moments. Barring this, you know you can't go too wrong with 97.1's breakfast with the Beatles (it's the *Beatles*, folks!) show on Sundays from eight A.M. to noon; or Merrill Schindler's show (5–7 P.M., Saturdays and Sundays), which takes a good look at all the city's best and worst eateries.

If these don't work, try flipping around—you'll be sure to come across a Spanish-language station or two playing some upbeat stuff for bored souls.

A Ghost and a Sci-fi Novel

Inspired by one science-fiction book and a setting for another futuristic film, *Blade Runner*, the Bradbury Building is a city treasure having the historic classification to back it up. Too, it has a wondrous Horatio Algeresque story behind it, steeped slightly in the paranormal. Lewis Bradbury, a California mining magnate, disappointed with the building plans given to him by established architect Sumner Hunt in 1892, conscripted Hunt's draftsman to try his hand. Reluctant at first, George Wyman and his wife consulted a Ouija-like board and apparently contacted Wyman's brother, who had been dead for some years. "Take Bradbury Building," was the deceased brother's ghastly advice. "It will make you famous." And that, as they say, was that. Inspired by *Looking Backward*, an old sci-fi book by Edward Bellamy describing a Utopian world circa 2000, Wyman took to heart the words describing a building therein as a "vast hall full of light, received not alone from the buildings on all sides, but from the dome. . . ." And he created a magnificent edifice to match, which looks pretty nondescript—except for its plaque— from the outside, but which is phenomenally beautiful on the inside as ornate black cast-iron gratings and elevator fixtures mesh synchronously with the tan wooden floors. A beautiful glow from the skylight above completes the mystical aura. Tourists are allowed only on the first floor; though, apparently, if you give the guard a few bucks (either as a bribe or, as the guard said, to go to a building restoration fund—we're not sure which), you can take the futuro-Victorian elevator to the top and walk down the Bradbury's steps and through its echoey halls.

The Bradbury Building
304 S. Broadway, Los Angeles
(213) 626-1893

Starving Artists at the Brewery

It might behoove any student or member of the ordinary job force to take a stroll through the ArtWalk at the Brewery when the on-site residents host their open house. If for no other reason, come to be inspired. The art colony hosts this free, on-premises ArtWalk, where hundreds of resident artists become vulnerable, allowing the estranged foot traffic of common passersby the chance to view (and/or purchase) their art. Since 1982, the public has been invited twice a year into the studios and ateliers of these artists to see firsthand what subcultures are thriving outside of manic office politics and the world of megacorporations. These abstractionists, painters, sculptors, and surrealists are intriguing to the core, and a great many of their works belong in museums. There are also restaurants and shops at the Brewery, and plenty of existential conversation. The Brewery is located where the Interstate 5 and Main Street meet. Visit www.breweryart.org for upcoming ArtWalks and other events sponsored by the Brewery Art Association.

A Nap Among the Greats

Kerouac admittedly napped a lot in college, and most scientists agree that we all need at least eight hours a night to function properly. Don't believe us? Well, that's all right. If you want proof of our claims, you can always stop by downtown L.A.'s Central Library, a wonderful structure that houses all the above info and more in its four glassy levels. In addition, it has a nice array of changing exhibits. (Last year's *Wizard of Oz* memorabilia showing was awesome!) The best thing about the library are the comfy chairs in the literature wing, as well as the plush grass out front. Yeah, yeah, of course all the books are nice . . . especially the big ones that block out the sun or the indoor fluorescent lighting. What we like to do is grab one of these, check it out, sit down, begin with the first few pages, and fall fast asleep. When we wake up, there are always plenty of Freud tomes around to tell us what our dreams meant.

Central Library
630 W. Fifth Street, Downtown
(213) 228-7000

An Idyllic Paradise . . . Almost

Los Angeles oil baron Edward L. Doheny bought this 22-acre parcel of land for his son in 1914. On it, a 55-room Tudor home was built in honor of Junior's wedding. Junior moved in with his wife and, tragically, he was fatally shot by his assistant a scant few months later. The assistant then turned the gun on himself, freezing the mystery in time forever. These days, the city of Beverly Hills maintains the beauteous and calming grounds of Greystone Mansion and its gardens, which are open to the public all week. One can walk through a pretty series of steps leading to various lush areas, including a well-groomed row of shrubbery where squirrels play happily. On a lower level, a gigantic pool (now filled in) sat, and there are a few stagnant, algae-filled fountains (and a mini-pond) housing tiny goldfish and the bigger, koi variety. The house itself is not open to the public, but one can peer in its windows to see the classy black-and-white-tiled flooring and an ornate banister leading upstairs. From the top of the grounds, where the parking lot is located, you may almost feel as though you are nowhere near a smog-ridden city until you let your eyes wander over the horizon. Below is all of L.A., which is beautiful in itself (though the gigantic billboard of Britney Spears [at time of publication] plastered on the side of one building tends to break the spell).

Greystone Mansion
905 Loma Vista Drive, Beverly Hills
(310) 550-4796

Political Intrigue and Lunch Among Monks

In the exhibit room at the Hsi Lai Buddhist Temple ($1 for entry), there's an amorphous mass of a white glittery substance that looks like a mineral, but is supposedly the "relic" of an ancient enlightened master—that is, the remains of said master after he was cremated. At Columbia College in New York City, one can occasionally see what remains of the ex–vice president and losing presidential candidate Al Gore, now an amorphous and hirsute (and very white, though not glittery) journalism professor. The connection? Well, there is none, really, though the Hsi Lai in Hacienda Heights (about twenty minutes northeast of Los Angeles) is the infamous spot where, in 1996, all those iniquitous Democratic Party donations were received (but Al Gore doesn't know about that—*really*). And though from certain angles, the Temple still looks like it's all about the money—shaven-headed Buddhist nuns sit at tables outside the main temple, processing donation checks; and "Dharma words" (karmic advice tucked away in crackable plastic balls) can be had from a machine, for four shiny quarters—it's certainly still a 14-acre spiritual encounter with chanting, burning incense, and calming gardens featuring lifelike statues of bygone arhats and the like. And the buildings themselves are a gorgeous shrine to that most nonviolent of religions—so be respectful when you're wandering the grounds or dining at the $5 all-you-care-to-eat vegetarian buffet (offered daily), taking in a class, or enjoying the tearoom. For, in the end, at least you can be pretty sure where your money is going this time around. And so the circle of life turns. . . .

Hsi Lai Buddhist Temple
3456 S. Glenmark Drive, Hacienda Heights
(626) 961-9697

This Ain't No Map to the Stars

Forget those cheesy overpriced photo tours for gossip hounds and the "Maps to the Stars Homes," which usually only lead you to well-fortified gates and views of overgrown front-yard shrubbery. If you want a real taste of our city, look to the Los Angeles Conservancy, a 6,500-member–strong, nonprofit organization established in 1978 and dedicated to keeping the city's history intact (and out of the hands of would-be developers who would bulldoze any available land—historically important or not—at the drop of a hat). Besides its watchdog duties, the Conservancy offers ten different guided walking tours of various historical aspects of Los Angeles at rock-bottom prices. For $8, non-members (tours are free for members) can take a nice stroll noting all of our Art Deco wonders or our terra-cotta buildings; or take an insider's look at Union Station. Just these three examples alone, you must admit, certainly beat trying to catch a glimpse of *Saturday Night Live*'s Rob Schneider at Skybar, or spending upward of $30 for one of those Hollywood bus tours, any day.

Los Angeles Conservancy Walking Tours
For more information, call (213) 623-2489
Or go to www.laconservancy.org

The Lizard King Was Here

Thousands of commuters make the trek over Laurel Canyon Boulevard every day. And as they pass the Canyon Country Store, they're also passing Love Street, although they may not be aware. Today, Jim Morrison's former home is a beautiful house with a redwood exterior, a huge deck, and a 20-foot window which used to showcase a totem pole carved with the likenesses of legendary greats Jimi Hendrix, John Lennon, Janis Joplin, and Jim Morrison. Several years ago it was a ramshackle wreck, with only the spray-painted "Mr. Mojo Rising" along the cement foundation to hint at its former glory. Painstakingly refurbished by Benjamin Lucas over the course of a few years, it's now a jewel. Recently sold to new owners, the totem pole is gone. Which is too bad, as it made a nice backdrop for all those Doors aficionados who came to the canyon with their cameras.

Jim Morrison's former home
8021 Rothdell Trail, Laurel Canyon

"Hey, Kid . . . Want to Fly?"

The Santa Monica Airport is more than a plane hangar for Scientology evangelists and corporate liners. It is also the home to an engrossing nonprofit aviation center called The Museum of

Flying. Check it out while, within shouting distance, loud jets take off into the stratosphere. The multilevel museum is a collective history of aviation from its beginnings through to the present, with info-spouting curators placed all around. There are models of World War Two planes such as the P-51 and the P-40 to look at, while resident curator and veteran Frank Jackson, the most sweet-natured, sincere hero anywhere around, takes you back to 1944 and shows pictures of the scene. One of the more sensational attractions is the *Venturer II* flight simulator on the first floor, enabling a simpleton like you the realistic illusion of being airborne. Of course, there are lots of aircraft to get up close and personal with, including the Supermarine Spitfire MK-14, or a Messerschmitt BF-109, or even a Hughes OH-6 Cayuse helicopter. Don't know what those are? Me neither (*chuckle, chuckle*), but it's fun to write about it as if I did! Also learn about those famous Wright brothers, who had a large hand in the invention of flight, as well as about the Space Shuttle, or listen to the air-traffic control on designated phones. So much to do for a meager suggested donation of $7 ($5 seniors; $3 children). Open Wednesday–Sunday, 10 A.M.–5 P.M.

The Museum of Flying
2772 Donald Douglas Loop North, Santa Monica
(310) 392-8822

The Days of Black-and-White Argon

Probably more relevant in Las Vegas than downtown Los Angeles, the Museum of Neon Art (MONA) is still fascinating for those generally curious about how things work. A prominent neon sign proclaims, "The true artist helps the world by revealing mystic truths," as you walk in, and what small wonders the last century of neon have provided—truly! This is not a large museum with umpteen exhibits and rooms to see; rather it is a convenient little art quarter that can be thoroughly walked through in a half hour's time, seeing the best in electric media. The building, which is in the Renaissance Tower, has legendary neon signs around the parameter, showcasing vintage Hollywood, including the old Brown Derby restaurant sign, dating back to 1929. MONA shows approximately eight to twelve exhibits a year, from historical and technical displays to group shows. To read through the history of neon is fascinating, and you will learn that krypton, xenon, and argon are more than planetary evils in the universe of science fiction and comic books; that they are among the rarer gases that carry an electric current. All the beer companies throughout the world should bow religiously to this one-of-a-kind museum, as if it were Mecca. Free parking beneath Renaissance Tower.

Museum of Neon Art (MONA)
501 West Olympic Boulevard, Los Angeles
(213) 489-9918

My Granddaddy Worked on the Railroad

If you are nutty about American railroad history, like the former Amtrak employees and walking encyclopedias that authored *Resident Tourist*, you must go to Griffith Park's Travel Town Museum. Originally designed to be a "railroad petting zoo" in the early 1950s, Travel Town displays sixteen different locomotives that date back some 140 years. Check out the massive Western Pacific No. 26, weighing in at 119 tons, which was built in 1909 by the American Locomotive Company, or the feathery Stockton Terminal and Eastern No. 1 (also called Mariposa), a 33-ton engine that was made in 1864. Each locomotive contains fascinating history, for the enthusiast and the greenhorn alike. And hell, they look nice because of fresh coats of paint courtesy of the museum. Travel Town also has cabooses, passenger cars, interurbans, and motorcars on display, some of which were purchased as scrap and reconstructed. One note of interest: The Travel Town location was a POW camp for Japanese, German, and Italian prisoners during World War Two, and the historic references to this plot go farther back still . . . but we'll leave some things for you to discover on your trip there. The museum is free to the public. Perfect for a family outing.

Travel Town Museum
5200 Zoo Drive, Griffith Park
(323) 662-5874

CHAPTER 8

Neighborhoods of Los Angeles

I Don't See Watts the Problem? (A Defense of Watts)

FOREWORD: *In 1978, just thirteen years removed from the 1965 inner-city riots—or "rebellions," as they were rightly referred to at the time— Watts underwent a radical change at the unassuming behest of a milk-skinned visionary and former NBA basketball player. You see, that year ex–Chicago Bull Ken Reeves moved into a troubled Watts community, acting on the persuasion of Carver High School principal and former teammate, Jim Willis. Reeves was hand-selected by Willis to coach the bas-ketball team, and moreover, to be a positive role model to students at Carver, thus steering them away from the temptation of crime. The new coach was a patient white man and a do-gooder, who resembled handsome former Denver Nuggets kingpin Dan Issel in ruddy complexion and cheekbone. For the next three years Watts became a televised allegory, and, more essentially, the basketball team at Carver High began to jell. (They won a great many close games; games they should have lost!) You may recall the apropos nickname issued Reeves in those days of deviance and moral folly. He was called, simply, "The White Shadow."*

Tsk, tsk. We are some twenty-one years removed from that golden era of CBS television, and yet the city of Watts is still held in low esteem. What a gol'-darn travesty. So here's what: Sick of defending San Fernando Valley locations and the already fully embraced wonders of Duarte, I became rabidly obsessed with shedding some positive light on the city of Watts. Something forceful needed to be documented. Therefore I have taken this occasion to point out the inner beauty of the inner city. Let me correct your fallacious image of this fair town. Indeed, let me rewire your basic thinking, because, "Hey, ya'll, this glass is half-full, yo." I decided against better judgment to take a trek or two to the condemned city in broad daylight to see if, indeed, it was as bad as people speculate. After all, I had always been fascinated with the Watts Towers, and from what I had heard, the library was a cornerstone of positive activity, decked to the tens with creamy pastels and leather bindings.

Watts has always seemed to be the bastard inner-city "'hood," the "projects," the "wrong side of town," when referred to in local and national news. Today Watts has monopolized the geographical role of villain. The name carries a certain irreparable stigma; it cannot be denied. We are warned of its violence and hoodlumry through media, cinema, and, of course, those poor neglected kids in rural America who try and harden their reputation by making outrageous claims like, "I was born in Watts, look out for me, sucker." Your reply to that should be: "Scary stuff, Ice-Wannabe, I have never been there, but *Resident Tourist* tells me it's nice." It helps our book's sales, and the adolescent dreamer will be hard-pressed to form a good comeback. But I am digressing.

The point is this: Without ever stepping foot in Watts, we common people conjecture that the streets are filled with machine guns and dope, gangs and uncivilized folk, anarchists and stray dogs. I gleaned on my first visit that this is simply untrue. There are no anarchists to speak of.

Still, we think "Watts," we think of trouble. We think of looters and crazy 1970s Jeri-curl. Asking a tourist to go see the Watts Towers is out of the question, because we are like baby birds that can only swallow half-masticated food that is fed to us from stronger-beaked birds.

I say, "Time to chew on your own, chicken. You have not lived until you have seen Watts."

Let us start from the beginning: A Mexican family purchased a plot of land where Watts now stands, and the area became known at that time as Ranch Tajuata, after the resident immigrants. This lasted for many years, and was changed only as the emergence of the electrical railroad burgeoned. Mr. Watts, a businessman and also a resident of the area, would take the train to work, and when he was dropped off back at home the conductor would yell out, "Watts!" The name stuck after a while, with people relating to the conductor. Mr. Watts, it can be surmised without speculation, would be very proud today that his name connotes such diversity forever linked to famous infamy. Anyway, Watts was officially annexed by Los Angeles in 1926, and City Hall was there even before that, with the foreboding words: "Towns are something like people. They can live up to a good name easier than they can live down a bad one." That's all Coach Reeves was trying to say to the kin all those years later, to no apparent avail.

Around this time, in the 1920s, the first store opened: Kellogg's. That's right, Tony the Tiger, Corn Flakes, picture-perfect moments. Postcards, Bridges of Madison County, stringing popcorn, and soft mittens. All of that. In 1920, one of Watts' most famous residents moved in and began what was to become the "architectural wonder" known as the Watts Towers. His name was Simon Rodia. The scrawny Italian immigrant worked for thirty-four years, in his *spare time*, to erect the three towers and the *Ship of Marco Polo*, an adjoining structure that looks like a ship, using no blueprints, no power tools, no scaffolding. He *did*, however, use broken 7-Up bottles, seashells, colorful stones, California art pottery, milk of magnesia bottles, and tool fragments, along with steel mesh and concrete borders. All of this was constructed by Simon, using a window-washer's belt and his bare hands. The tallest tower is 99'6" tall. That is 94'6" taller than Simon Rodia. Simon died in 1965, but his inspirational towers still stand harrowingly tall on 107th Street, having survived fires, earthquakes (namely the 1933 Long Beach quake, which ruined a great many buildings farther away), and the occasional riot. That is some pretty enduring artwork. "I had in mind to do something big, and I did," he said, shortly after his project was complete, and we have been wassailing him ever since with 40-ouncers. These phenomenal structures should obliterate any fear and prejudice we may harbor. They are a California and National Historic Landmark. (NOTE: The "stray" dogs roaming the area there likely belong to somebody, and are generally harmless to doddering elderly people. There are not even very many people on the sidewalks, at least ones who are conscious.)

The Watts Towers are the greatest attraction in the city, but there are many other aspects of this fine community worth noting. Firstly, Watts has a sense of hair-raising desertion. It is perpetually under the haze of a silver-hued "marine layer" (or smog, as it's known to asshole realists). The total parameter of Watts is four square miles, but it seems to stretch out forever. Watts is precisely centralized in the city of Los Angeles. It rests smack in the middle of South-Central Los Angeles, much like Van Nuys does in the San Fernando Valley, with no wooded areas, no rivers, no streams or ponds. No natural water bodies means *no disease-carrying mosquitoes!* That's right, you are safer in Watts from getting mosquito bites than virtually anywhere in the United States, including Pittsburgh. Any trees or shrubbery you see in Watts are transplants, artificial or otherwise—get what I am saying? One of the greatest homemade rose gardens can be found in Watts, started by Dorothy Simpson. It is called the Watts Senior Center Rose Garden, and has nearly five hundred rosebushes, and the aroma of a million. Not bad for a place that lacks natural vegetation. The town is 100 feet above sea level, and there is less rainfall in Watts than in downtown Los Angeles, exactly 7¾ miles away. There is more fog (smog, marine layer, what-have-you), though, and stronger winds coming from the shores of Redondo Beach where, as everybody knows, the Beach Boys once had a concert. But wait—there's more!

Did you know that jazz legend and composer Charles Mingus graduated from high school in Watts? Well, he did, and he didn't seem to have too much trouble coping in society, now, did he? He isn't the only one, either. Buddy Collett also emerged from Watts, as did San Francisco 49er Joe Perry, and Joe Adams, the first black disc jockey, and Dorothy Doakes, the first black student to get a scholarship to UCLA. Watts was also the home of the first-ever women's jury in the United States, making it a bit of a pioneering town.

Okay, you're into theology but fear Watts won't have a place of worship suited to your needs. Not so! There are ten denominational churches in Watts, including Baptist, Methodist, Presbyterian, Episcopal, Methodist Episcopal, Free Methodist, Christian, Christian Science, Catholic, and others. That is a whole lot of God, represented by some of the city's finest evangelists. Buddhists are welcome, as are agnostics and Satanists. After services, there is excellent fresh catfish served at Jordan's Food Center. There's nothing like the taste of fried catfish after learning about eternal rewards and/or perdition. They are hand and hand (the catfish and religion, not rewards and perdition).

I know, I know. All this coloring and embellishment without mention of the gangs that surfaced in the vicinity of Watts, and the recent 1992 riots after the Rodney King verdict. First things first: So what if the Crips and Bloods were invented in Watts, they are as ghostly as our common ancestors today (although there are still a few around). Territory was at a premium back in the day, and, much like the stock market, things changed. Territory is down five points. Harmony is up. And hey, not all history is proud in any given city. Besides, the Crips came out of Fremont High School, outside of Watts. It is centrally located, so the convenient meeting place was, naturally, Watts. As far as we know, both gangs have disbanded forever, and the truce is still on. Bygones are bygones. Today former members of each gang (now sporting sunshine-yellow colors to signify their newest gang—the Get-Along Gang) enjoy cheese and wine together at neighborhood strengthening sessions (or, at least they should, you Wonder Bread reader). The Rodney King thing was a shame, but at the time it seemed cool for people to loot and stuff. We are human beings, and we are instinctual. Besides, did you see how much Mr. Kim was charging for that ghetto blaster? Outrageous! Looting was the only way to get it in the low-income neighborhood. The total damage was one billion dollars' worth of repairs after that, with fifty-two people killed and some sixteen thousand arrested, which is not nearly so bad when matched up against the population of the entire state of California. These people were of all colors and races. Some of them had mothers. Can you imagine?

Just don't go there after dark.

Hollywood Is Not a City That Changes

Hollywood—that vague stretch of L.A. city property that finds its de facto center somewhere near Graumann's Chinese Theater on Hollywood Boulevard, is not a city; never has been. No, what began as a basic ploy to get people to buy real estate here, has become just another—albeit a famous (in many cases, infamous) one—incorporated area of greater Los Angeles with only an honorary mayor and vague borders.

"It depends on who you ask," said Anne Steams, director of tourism for the Hollywood Chamber of Commerce, a non-governmental organization which promotes business in the incorporated region that is known as Hollywood. "The Hollywood CRA [Community Redevelopment Agency], kind of thinks of Hollywood in a really large sense. And then we have the Hollywood Business Improvement District that kind of just looks at it as being just the historic area of Hollywood Boulevard. And as kind of a loose rule, we tend to think of it as south to Melrose, north to the [Hollywood] Hills, west to maybe Fairfax, and then east . . . all the way up to Vermont." (Blvd., that is.)

Tourists, for their part, tend to get to know Hollywood as the currently grimy little track of Hollywood Boulevard running from Mann's Chinese Theater to, say, the Frederick's of Hollywood store farther east. The other thing tourists often end up thinking about Hollywood, is that—with its numerous chintzy "3 shirts for $10" stores, its collection of schlocky museums (Guinness, Ripley's, the Wax Museum), its tattoo parlors, and its amalgam of bold panhandlers—it's a bit of a dirty disappointment. *Where's all the glamour, all the movie stars?* one may think to himself as he walks by the group of punky young kids eternally stationed in front of the McDonald's, near the corner of Highland; or as he steps over the crippled man dutifully wiping the Walk of Fame stars clean. But then, unbeknownst even to many residents here, the star-cleaner, whose real name is John Peterson, actually represents to some degree the changing face of Hollywood. Ostensibly just another homeless person on the boulevard, Peterson is, in fact, not homeless at all. When Hollywood's business-improvement district, known as the Hollywood Entertainment District, opened up contracting bids for a new street-cleaner a couple of years back, they set down a precedent having to do with Peterson, who, up until then, had been homeless, and was doing his work for those certain Boulevard shops who would pay him. "One of the conditions of getting the contract is that they bring him on board and pay him a salary," said an Entertainment District spokesperson. And so today, Peterson has a forty-hour-a-week job and an apartment through the help of Hollywood itself.

The changes are much less subtle than this, though. One only has to look at the hulking new Hollywood and Highland development, with its giant Gap outlet and, inside, its fresh, white elephant statues overlooking a multistory mall, to see that—as one wise singer once said, not about L.A.—that "the times, they are a-changin'." This new structure, which butts up against the recently installed subway station here, hosted the Oscar ceremonies at its Kodak Theater in 2002, thus taking the event away from the Shrine Auditorium (where it had been held for many years), and effectively bringing it back to the area from whence the Oscars came (the first Academy Awards, a much smaller affair than now, were held in 1929 in the Roosevelt Hotel, across the street from Mann's). But change—even under the supposed guise of improvement—doesn't always bring satisfaction. Yes, certainly some people will miss Hollywood's old urban edginess made famous by such bands as Guns 'N Roses, who did a video here in the late '80s for their aptly titled tune "Welcome to the Jungle." As one L.A. resident said about the Highland and Hollywood development: "It was such a disappointment. It's just a mall." And, as tattered buildings and junky tourist-traps selling reproduced photos of Leonardo DiCaprio, Brad Pitt, and the like make way for Banana Republics and Neutrogena product stands; and as some local folk clamor for a Hollywood independent of Los Angeles (just as the Valley has its own secessionist movement); and while Mayor Jim Hahn vows to keep Hollywood a part of L.A.— it's tough to say what Hollywood's new identity will entail, exactly. The truth of the matter is twofold: Hollywood, as the tourists see it now, is sleazier than it once was. But this is changing, for good or bad, by the day—the minute, even.

The very least anyone can hope for the area is that Britney

Spears doesn't someday do a song about Hollywood called "Welcome to the Shopping Center."

Cahuenga Is for Music Lovers

When the sun is out, this little block of land betwixt Sunset and, say, Fountain, seemingly only offers a giant open-air magazine kiosk (foreign-language readers and eclectic porn lovers, take note) and a corner Popeye's Chicken outlet. At night, however, as turntables begin to light up and the occasional group of avant-garde minstrels takes the stage at the Hotel Café, the transformation into funkiness begins. At Beauty Bar (see chapter 2), David Bowie and Hüsker Dü play in the background amid 1960s-era hair dryers as Hollywood yokels do their best latter-day Rat Pack and Rat Pack mole imitations. Folks displaying post-punk malaise in leather jackets and beat-up jeans pack themselves tightly into **The Burgundy Room** (1621½ Cahuenga Boulevard) for the Stranglers and Blondie spun by jean-jacketed DJs. And if white-bred rock and roll ain't your thing, then, after crossing through the back alley entrance to **The Room** (1626 Cahuenga Boulevard), you can sip cocktails at a mellow red-lighted bar with slicker L.A. types and, on most nights, listen to hip-hop or dance being spun. The best part about it all is that in such an automobile-centric city as L.A., you can, if you want (rumors have it that some residents, too L.A. for their own good, feel a strong desire to get in their car just to move to a new location across the street), park in one place and spend the night on drunken foot—yes, you heard it here: drunken foot.

Cahuenga Boulevard, between Hollywood and Fountain

The Magic Fountain and More

L.A.'s Chinatown—a dusty, odorific couple of rows (the main ones being North Broadway and North Spring Street) consisting of numerous restaurants and eclectic tourist shops carrying everything from fine vases to Buddha figurines to boxes of those little Hershey's Kiss–shaped children's poppers—has seen better days, but we still dig it for its spent charm. During the weekends especially, it comes alive as people of all ethnic groups shop—among old, well-dressed, chain-smoking Chinese men and the occasional team of plate-balancers—for bargain polyester-blend clothing, jewelry, veggies, as well as traditional Chinese restorative herbs like ginseng and the like. Of special interest is the Chinese wishing-well where tourists can throw their change through a gate and into pots encrusted in cement: Make a basket, and there you'll have it, money or luck or even a long life. Or save your coinage and simply enjoy the turtles swimming around in the fountain's algae-full pool. Around the corner from there is **Hop Louie** (950 Mei Ling Way), a terraced Chinese restaurant with an eerie, traditional feel. We're sure the food is fine; however, the real draw is the bar, which at nighttime awakens with a mixture of old-timers and young, goateed, literary-looking types. And speaking of the nighttime, this area, though underappreciated for the shady feel it takes on after dusk, has a goodly amount of fun in store for the brave-hearted. **Grand Star Restaurant** (943 Sun Mun Way) is another time-warped restaurant/bar (serving tasty fruit concoctions) of nice distinction. On the first and third Friday of every month, Star offers Firecracker, a cracking good club, which for its multiracial crowd, sometimes feel like a danceable Americana. As well, a group of ultramodern galleries have opened in the Chinatown Plaza under a row of faded lanterns, offering the occasional nighttime walk-and-look-and-drink. Stumbling home, be sure to walk back by the fountain to see how the coins "magically" disappear before morning.

Chinatown
Downtown

Nighthawks on Fairfax

A harmless Jewish-community shopping street by day, Fairfax Avenue becomes the place to be for the city's sundry nighthawk types when the sun goes down. At dusk, the bars—Max's, a dark little bar with special mint drinks; Largo, a supper club with a nice range of performers including locals Aimee Mann and her husband, Michael Penn; and The Kibitz Room (see chapter 2 listings), the dive bar attached to Canter's, come alive, and out come the coffee- and booze-soaked zombies. But it's after two A.M. that things really get crawling. This eerie little strip between Melrose and Beverly features Canter's Restaurant and Delicatessen, open twenty-four hours for those insomniacs who have a hankering for lifeblood-giving matzo-ball soup (the Thanksgiving dinner, among other things, is for all you gentiles). Across the street is the strangely non-ambient Damiano's Pizza, which still seems to pack them in until after three in the morning (it certainly has nothing to do with the second-run boxes advertising every pizza place but their own they give you for your to-go orders). The pizza is greasily satisfying as a preemptive strike on a hangover, and the benches outside are always a great place to gather to meet swaying cigarette-bummers or to practice your Russian-listening comprehension with the Damiano's delivery dudes. Harry Blitzstein, the street's nighthawk artist-in-residence is a property manager by day and an oil paint–mad artist by night; if you're lucky, you might catch a glimpse of him even after his Blitzstein Museum of Art closes; and if you praise his work through the glass, he's been known to give a nice little bow. At Nova Express Café the coffee is good and strong, which will keep you up yet another few hours, before the sun rises and it's time to go to bed.

Fairfax Avenue, between Melrose and Beverly Boulevard, Los Angeles
Max's
442 N. Fairfax Avenue

Largo
423 N. Fairfax Avenue
Damiano's Pizza
412 N. Fairfax Avenue
Blitzstein Museum of Art
430 N. Fairfax Avenue
Nova Express Café
426 N. Fairfax Avenue

Franklin Avenue Is for Lovers

One of Los Angeles' tidiest little strips of commerce is located on Franklin Avenue at Tamarind, where a rather stylish coffeehouse called—appropriately enough—the Bourgeois Pig sits most engagingly; anything carrying that moniker is okay with us. Cozy booths, a pool table, an outdoor patio, tripped-out music, and fecund artwork make up this ambient lounge, a perfect place to duck into from a sweltering sun. The beauty of the whole area is in the serenity of the surrounding hillocks, which are green and dense, and somewhat calming. Directly next door is a kind of New Age bookshop called The Daily Planet that sells all sorts of magazines, aromatherapy devices, candles, chimes, and various activist materials—all the soft touches to starting a revolution. On the other side of the Bourgeois Pig, there is a college-type bar with televisions and wooden booths called Birds, which has the cross-integration of downtrodden drunks and celebrity types alike. The beers are relatively affordable, and the atmosphere is not filled with the usual Hollywood tensions; rather it has the fundamental air of jettisoned sobriety. What a release! Or there is also *Resident Tourist*'s favorite used-book and -record store, a little farther east of Birds, called Counterpoint Records and Books. This place is marginally organized; it's easy to locate what you're looking for, and has all the literature, poetry, art, history, and philosophy books you could want—all very inexpensive. (Can you really put a price tag on good literature?) There's also a staggering selection of dust-free classical, jazz, rock, and folk records, bringing back to mind that lovely staple of our 1970s youth—Peaches.

Bourgeois Pig
5931 Franklin Avenue, Hollywood
(323) 464-6008
The Daily Planet
593½ Franklin Avenue, Hollywood
(323) 957-0061
Birds
5925 Franklin Avenue, Hollywood
(323) 465-0175
Counterpoint Records and Books
5911 Franklin Avenue, Hollywood
(323) 957-7965

Hollywood Boulevard Has Its Appeal

For years, Hollywood Boulevard has always been a destination for starry-eyed hordes, despite the fact that, other than Graumann's Chinese Theater, there wasn't a whole lot to see or do. The junky charm of the souvenir shops lining either side didn't really provide much fulfillment in the street-of-dreams department (with the exception of **Hollywood T-shirts**, see chapter 10). That's all changed—and how! The Hollywood and Highland Complex, which houses the Kodak Theater, the new home for the Oscars, brought with it a huge revitalization of the area. It's a massive maze of retail and restaurant, and the Metro stop right below does make it awfully convenient to get there. There's lots that's bright and shiny and new, as of November 2001, and, since they built it, they will come. And when they do, I hope they'll head east for a couple of blocks, because there are still some gems from the old days down that way. Musso and Frank's is a must-stop for a martini; no ifs, ands, or buts, you simply must belly-up to the bar or slide into a red leather booth and experience the Musso and Frank martini. If it's still around breakfast time, pair it with some of their famous flannel cakes, and you're primed for the day. Musso's is truly an old Hollywood treasure, a revered old watering hole, famous for deals made and stars seen. The waiters have been there for about a hundred years and they're fazed by nothing. The menu covers pretty much everything you could want, à la carte, and for some reason, the plain old water they serve is absolutely delicious. Must be filtered or something, because it doesn't taste like tap. If it's Friday, get the clam chowder. That and the half-loaf of sourdough bread put on your table should fill you up. Oh, and maybe a side of mashed potatoes. Load up on those carbs, and keep your eyes open for stars! Supply Sergeant is stocked with scores of military accoutrements, and it can be used for a lot of things, ranging from camping to survival. Mess kits, canteens, gloves, rocket launchers, gas masks—the items run the gamut from essential to useful to frightening. You can pick up patches from foreign countries, and for those few cold days south-ern California manages to muster up in the winter, you should grab some gloves. Caps, shirts, T's, lots of camouflage, and standard-issue line the shelves. You'll find duffel bags *and* body bags, knives, flashlights, all sorts of survival gear. A few doors down is Frederick's of Hollywood, where you can both buy today's fashions and browse through lingerie history. Downstairs, it's a retail store, featuring lots of imaginative bras, teddies, and bikinis, both risqué and utilitarian. If you're in desperate need of a boa-trimmed chiffon chemise, this is your place. Velvet? Lace? Lots to be found. And for sexy footwear in and out of the bed-room, Frederick's has a fine selection of candy-colored mules, trimmed in feathers. Also available are Lucite slip-ons, with sky-high platforms and heels, in vibrant colors. Upstairs is the Lin-gerie Museum with sights such as Madonna's cone bra from the Material Girl tour and Tom Hanks' underwear from *Forrest Gump,* as well as classics like the bra Tony Curtis wore in *Some Like it Hot.* Other sights range from a metal breastplate worn by guitarist

Lita Ford on stage to lingerie worn by Marilyn Monroe, Greta Garbo, or Cybill Shepard in *Moonlighting*.

Musso and Frank's
667 Hollywood Boulevard, Hollywood
(323) 467-5123
Supply Sergeant
6664 Hollywood Boulevard, Hollywood
(323) 463-4730
Frederick's of Hollywood
6608 Hollywood Boulevard, Hollywood
(323) 466-5151
www.fredericks.com

La Brea, Too, but Just a Little Corner

La Brea Avenue is such that you could park on the corner of Santa Monica Boulevard and La Brea, walk and shop one side all the way down to Wilshire Boulevard, and be exhausted. It's wall-to-wall retail, furnishings, restaurants, vintage stores, art-supply stores, boutiques, and even a vintage hardware store. Both east and west sides are loaded with every kind of anything, so it's a good bet you'll spend some time here. We'll just cover a little corner, to give a taste of just how eclectic it is. First, two little stores, both with scores of special books, gifts, note cards, stationery, and more. Illiterature is the bookstore, and Pulp offers the stationery and cards, and they both feature a fine selection of accoutrements. Illiterature offers bath condiments, lotions, and great gift ideas, some kitschy, some classy, as well. Pulp is the store for the writer you know, or the one inside you. It's packed with paper, and just the kind of place to go when you need a gift and you have no ideas. You'll walk out with something. At once a florist and a café, Rita Flora is a wonderful break for a bite if you find yourself on La Brea Avenue. Rita Flora offers delicious soups, sandwiches, and salads in fragrant and beautiful surroundings. Sit outside at one of the sidewalk tables and watch some of the beautiful people shuf-fle by. Re-covering your dining-room chairs might not be on your mind as you make your way through all that L.A. has to offer, but maybe it should be. Diamond Foam has a great selection of magnificent materials that will make you want to reupholster your life. From rich brocades to basic canvas, or exotic silks, the selection here is wide and varied. Don't miss the remnants sec-tion. Remnants offer great prices for great pieces, and are just the right size to tuck in a suitcase for the trip home. The School Ser-vice Co. really takes you back. Whether or not you're a teacher, it's a wonderful ramble down memory lane, with all the big, col-orful wall posters, like *Germination of a Bean* and *Our Solar System*. Holiday stuff, textbooks, extracurricular items, and art supplies abound; it's a worthwhile look-see, and while a gift from here may not rank up there with a T-shirt that says, MY MOM WENT TO HOLLYWOOD AND ALL I GOT WAS THIS STUPID T-SHIRT, it will most likely be better used in the long run. This is also a good pit stop to pick up some essential items to have in the car for those long road trips. You'll find lots to keep little minds and hands occupied.

Illiterature and **Pulp**
452 S. La Brea Avenue, and 456 S. La Brea Avenue, Los Angeles
(323) 937-3505
(323) 937-3506
Rita Flora
468 S. La Brea Avenue, Los Angeles
(323) 938-3900
ritaflora.com
Diamond Foam and Fabric
611 S. La Brea Avenue, Los Angeles
(323) 931-8148
School Service Co.
647 N. La Brea Avenue, Los Angeles
(323) 933-5691

NEIGHBORHOODS OF LOS ANGELES

A Clean Place in the Dirty City

Hands-down, the Japanese win for the tidiest downtown area. This few-square-blocks area, starting near First and Alameda Streets, is like an immaculate and quaint Kyoto dream. Be sure to walk through the Japanese Village Plaza Mall, where you can eat noodles and buy imported getas, robes, or sweet bean cakes at the various shops. The Joy Mart offers some nice American-Japanese hybrid meals of french fries and noodles, as well as your favorite (but expensive) cold Japanese imported non-sweetened, canned coffees, which are a nice break from the sugary American versions. Maguro-Tei, on the second floor of the Little Tokyo Mall, is a fairly priced catchall restaurant with sushi, rice dishes, and a great Japanese salad bar, while East on First Street is a sushi/noodle shop with the warmest red glow this side of Tokyo. The Japanese American National Museum relays in a beautiful, modern setting the glories and tragedies of the Japanese-American experience (the history of World War Two Japanese Internment Camps is a brilliant and disheartening display). Also, be sure to visit the Koban (see next page), for L.A. and Little Tokyo tourist information. At night, the area takes on a comfortable tone (somehow, while the rest of downtown becomes sketchy at night, this little area seems to stay mostly on the up-and-up) as tourists and residents alike take eat and drink in the area's many karaoke (try the huge Oiwake in the Village Plaza Mall), sushi (Frying Fish, a nice revolving sushi shop, also in the Plaza, is a great experience), and noodle shops; do note that "Hirashimase" means welcome in Japanese, for you will hear this word just about every time you enter any shop serving food down here.

The Japanese rightfully (theirs is not a big country) have this thing about concise space: a bedroom with a futon can, once the futon is rolled up, easily become a living room. And sometimes bathrooms in Japan are no more than a heated (yes, they have a thing about their potties, too) toilet. And while we have our various jurisdiction police headquarters (which they do, too) spread all over, they also have convenient little rooms called Kobans, or police boxes, which act as mini–local cop shops, where locals can report purse-snatchings and malfeasances of all kinds. Fittingly (and not well known to most people outside of the immediate community), Little Tokyo has its own Koban. But while the usual handful of doughy cops—this seems to be a worldwide problem—are stationed at the ones in Japan, Little Tokyo's Koban is more of a community way station, where tourists of all kinds (but especially Japanese) can come and get information about the city and Little Tokyo, which, besides being very clean, has an abundance of tourist eye candy. As well, on certain weekday nights, the Koban hosts a language exchange, where Japanese can learn English and English speakers can practice their Japanese.

Little Tokyo's Koban
307 E. First Street, Los Angeles
(213) 613-0281

The Wester Is the Bester

L.A.'s famous Melrose Avenue, between La Brea and Fairfax, may be as much as a disappointment to tourists these days as the still-tacky (though becoming more gentrified by the day) Hollywood Boulevard. Still, this strip of Melrose, with its tennis-shoe shops, glammy-style clothing retailers, record stores, and quaint and expensive restaurants alike, is not without its chintzy charm. While there, do take note of **Wound & Wound Toy Company** (see chapter 10), as well as Red Balls on Fire, a warehouse clothing emporium for the raver in you; Urban Outfitters sells cheap though eternally hip clothing. Feel free, on the other hand, to ignore any shops that sell accessories having anything to do with Axl Rose (one leather shop, for the longest time, had in its window, a jacket with his bandannaed likeness painted on the back). And by all means, avoid the Strip's many tattoo parlors, unless of course, you're drunk. While drunk, also be sure to consider buying an overpriced vintage rock T-shirt—all the rage these days with the tragically trendy. If you do end up making such a purchase, you'll feel right at home at The Gig–Hollywood, a cool venue for L.A.'s megavanitized pop-rock bands. If not, The Snake Pit, with its great jukebox and pub charm, is a decent bet. A haute-ier experience can be had on this street, west of Fairfax. Dubbed "Melrose West," these few blocks have recently become known as a great retail experience. Located here is the antiseptic, two-story clothes warehouse, **Fred Segal**, kitty-corner from L.A. designer Emma Gold's **Miu Miu**. And nearby are boutiques by **Betsey Johnson**, **Daryl K**, swimwear designer **Liza Bruce**, and chic vintage at **Decades**. Farther west past La Cienega, Melrose takes on a more New Age, neighborhoody feel, as clothing outlets make way for galleries, furniture stores, and a nice coffee shop—Urth Café—stocked with script-reading aspiring actors. This is next door to the Bodhi Tree, L.A.'s finest self-help book and tape outlet; and nearby is Elixir, which is a gorgeous little Japanese garden masquerading as a café serving cures for hangovers, lethargy, and the like.

Melrose Avenue, from La Brea Avenue to La Cienega Boulevard

Red Balls on Fire
7365 Melrose Avenue, Hollywood
(323) 655-3409

Urban Outfitters
7650 Melrose Avenue, Hollywood
(323) 653-3231

The Gig–Hollywood
7302 Melrose Avenue, Hollywood
(323) 936-4440

The Snake Pit
7529 Melrose Avenue, Hollywood
(323) 653-2011

RESIDENT TOURIST: LOS ANGELES

Urth Café
8565 W. Melrose Avenue, Hollywood
(310) 659-0628
Bodhi Tree
8585 W. Melrose Avenue, Hollywood
(310) 659-1733
Elixir
8612 W. Melrose Avenue, Hollywood
(310) 657-9300
Mondo Video A-Go-Go
4328 Melrose Avenue, Hollywood
(323) 953-8896

By Any Other Name

Yes, we've taken into account the neat little moving walkway for grocery-cart holders at Ralph's, and still, this stretch of Wilshire, from La Brea to Fairfax, Miracle Mile, doesn't seem like much of a miracle anymore. Originally named for its 1920s heyday, those days are pretty much gone, leaving a mostly sorrowful little strip of video stores, commercial office buildings, office supply outlets, a Smart and Final, as well as a few conglomerations of restaurants for area worker-bees. (*Variety*, the *Los Angeles Business Journal*, and the American Federation of Television Artists are some of the organizations that hold offices here.) Still, Museum Row here continues to be a big tourist draw, with the Los Angeles County Museum of Art being quite popular; especially interesting is LACMA's wing, the Pavilion of Japanese Art, which treats its viewers to a low-impact spiral walk not unlike New York's Guggenheim Museum. As well, the Pavilion's collection of netsuke—ornately carved and quite tiny kimono sash-holders—is really cool for their ofttimes fantastic representations of monsters and gods and children playing. The Row also holds the Petersen Automotive Museum, the well-known primordial bubblings of the La Brea Tar Pits, and the Los Angeles Craft and Folk Art

Museum. Sadly, however, the Carol and Barry Kaye Museum of Miniatures closed its doors for good this year. Scant on nightlife, the so-called Miracle Mile nonetheless does hold one of L.A.'s premiere semi-intimate rock venues, the El Rey Theatre, which recently has had such acts as Badly Drawn Boy and Emmylou Harris. And once a month, the El Rey hosts the premiere glam **Club Makeup** (see chapter 2 listings), a mandatory experience for all David Bowie, Iggy Pop, and T. Rex fans of the open-minded variety. The Conga Room, too, has become a hot spot for fans of Latin music.

Miracle Mile
Wilshire Boulevard between Fairfax and La Brea Avenues, Los Angeles

Los Angeles County Museum of Art
5905 Wilshire Boulevard
(323) 857-6000

Petersen Automotive Museum
6060 Wilshire Boulevard
(323) 930-2277

Los Angeles Craft and Folk Art Museum
5814 Wilshire Boulevard
(323) 937-4230

El Rey Theatre
5515 Wilshire Boulevard
(323) 936-6400

The Conga Room
5364 Wilshire Boulevard
(323) 938-1696

Skid Row as a Drive-by Adventure
Skid Row, a downtown Los Angeles area where hundreds of homeless live in tents, in shelters, and even right there on the ground, says to the uninitiated, "Look, but don't touch." And we can't in good conscience advise you—despite our liberal lean-

ings—to pile the kids in the car with cameras and bottled water in tow to park there and walk through the areas of Fifth, Sixth, and Seventh Streets near the San Pedro crossing like common tourists (though *we* did, sans kids, which two of us don't have anyway). But if you're not one to be daunted by a little grime and poor living (or if you are feeling like your lot in life is at all bad), then we are not against you taking a guarded brisk stroll through this area during the daytime. (At night, you might do best, if driving through there, to have a full tank of gas; or, if walking, to have had some previous experience with a sheath or other makeshift weapon.) Besides possessing some of Los Angeles' most beautiful architecture (take note of the Hotel Alexandria, which once housed the likes of Charlie Chaplin for days on end, and has seen better ones), the little enclave on Fifth Street, especially, has plenty of dive bars (the King Edward Saloon, Charlie O's) where, if you're brave enough to stop in for a drink, you might end up coming out with a fine story to tell the bored people back home—many of the area's watering holes serve plenty of—how do you say?—eccentrics, after all. As well, if you tip nicely, the bartenders might tell you what movies the bigwigs in Hollywood made in this area, a common location for shoots. Of course, don't expect to necessarily stumble out of these places to get a breath of fresh air; in summer especially, the area tends to take on a pungent urine smell, despite (or because of) all the city Port-a-potties lining the sidewalks here.

Skid Row
Downtown Los Angeles

Take a Right at the Ocean

If Venice Beach is a nomad's paradise, then the short block of Washington Boulevard leading out onto the Venice pier is the perfect oasis for travelers here. This sand-blown street is an excellent launching point for seafarers as well as landlubbers intent on venturing farther into that otherworldly realm that is the incorporated area of Venice. And for that matter, as the sun begins to set into the ocean, Washington is also a great place to see the day end. The Venice Whaler, for example, is a comfy two-story dive where you can enjoy a plate of fish and chips on the patio during the day and fruity drinks with Hawaiian-shirted Jimmy Buffett fans and college folk at night. **Hinano** (see chapter 2 listings), too, has a mean burger and pool tables for wee-hour scratching, while the C & O Trattoria, a wonderful Italian place where they serve you big plates of pasta, family style, provides a hearty lunch, but really gets romantic after dusk. If you're intent on renting a bike or Rollerblades, however, it is pretty certain you'll have to return them before sundown. No big deal. By then, you'll be plenty ready to enjoy a cup of coffee or fruit drink at the Cow's End Café. If your express goal is Venice, however, just walk (or pedal or blade) toward the ocean and take a right at the self-explanatory Ocean Front Walk. It may take you a little while to get to all the cheese (sunglasses shops, bong stores, and greasy stands) that is the true Venice, but it's certain you'll be glad you began where you did; for, nestled on this little street, are all kinds of beautiful architectural small wonders, as well as houses that are odes to the area's general alternative tone. We'd warn you to look out for the Harmony House, but you're sure not to miss it, with its big fat Buddha sitting out front. Another example is the wondrous little number that, by its red lookout post, looks like it was made by someone who wasn't fortunate enough to have a tree fort as a kid. Keep going and soon enough you'll find yourself in the mad bazaar of Venice, that wondrous place made up of charm and dirt.

Washington Boulevard, Venice
The Venice Whaler
2-10 Washington Boulevard
C & O Trattoria
31 Washington Boulevard
Cow's End Café
34 Washington Boulevard

Tom Petty Made Ventura into a Legend

There are so many eclectic shopping nooks in the Southland, but for sheer range and length, you can't beat Ventura Boulevard. There is a mind-boggling amount of variety and it is simply too long to walk the entirety, but here's a sampling. If it's Sunday, the **Studio City Farmers' Market** is in full swing early on Ventura Place, a slice of a street that runs at an angle between Laurel Canyon and Ventura. Fresh produce, a petting zoo, and train rides, it's a lovely way to start the day. You might stop by to visit the dogs of the Brittany Foundation, a dog rescue group that holds adoption programs at the corner of Ventura and Laurel Canyon Boulevards each Sunday from 10:30 A.M. to 3 P.M. If you're a tourist, you'll have to be content with just petting, as they only adopt locally—a home check is the final step in the approval process. You'll not have far to traipse hungry or thirsty, as there is refreshment on every block. Snacks, gourmet meals, juice bars, burgers, whatever may be your craving, you'll find it within minutes. You can't go wrong with Carney's, a renovated train car renowned for its chili burgers, dogs, and fries. In fact, there's nothing wrong with a chili cheeseburger *and* chili fries to begin your trek.

The Psychic Eye Bookstore is where you'll find the harmonic convergence of psychic energy north of Mulholland. PARAPHERNA-LIA FOR ALL PERSUASIONS, reads a sign on the side of the building, and that covers a lot of persuasions: readings from any number of available psychics, held behind velvet curtains; classes on the psychic sciences; amulets for dowsing, to give you the answers; other amulets for fertility and sexual control; talismans, crystals, herbs, gemstones, incense, milagros—oh yes, and books, too. Key chains with aliens in a vial, and elaborate hookahs contribute to the array of extrasensory equipment. Astrology charts can be done in a day, which is great for a little guidance if you're only here for a short time. For a hoot, scoot on into the Vespa Shop. Yes, the Vespa shop. Ride polite or die, indeed. It's clean, glitzy fun, even if you don't ride out on a shiny new scooter. Who knew mods might ride again?

The Antique Mall in Sherman Oaks is like your grand-mother's attic, only much cleaner and better organized. Loads of booths fill the space, stocked with hundreds of items from days of yore. Costume jewelry, those ever-popular metal lunchboxes you wish you'd saved, clothing, toys—this place was made for wandering. Vintage-hounds and collectors will want to make a stop here.

Iguana Vintage Clothing offers lots of room to roam in this spacious, well-laid-out store. There's room between the racks for more than one person, for starters. And the store is stocked with real quality merchandise, everything in nearly mint condition. It's a tad pricey, but still not so bad compared to some of the places over the hill. Jeans, eyelet and rayon dresses, cocktail gowns, and lots of lamé make this place worth dropping some cash. There are pageboy wigs of every hue, a great selection of sunglasses and frames, shoes (lots of Chuck Taylor's), and upstairs, where things are quite reasonably priced, you'll find a terrific selection of shirts, tops, suits (the women's suits were great), and pants.

Already hungry again? How about another burger? You can never have enough burgers. This time, let's make it a Fatburger. The chain was recently acquired by Magic Johnson, and let's hope he doesn't change a thing. Fatburger is a 47-store chain, with locations in California, Nevada, Arizona, and Washington. With Magic's purchase, there are extensive expansion plans in the works. If you're really hungry, order the King Burger. It's huge, and you can add an egg, bacon, or chili to this monster, or any other burger. Add an order of fries, fat or skinny, and you're set. You can also get a turkey burger or a hot dog, but why bother here? The chili can't top Carney's, so keep it pure. Fatburger bills itself as "The Last Great Hamburger Stand," and it's all fresh, right down to the fresh-squeezed lemonade. Also fresh are the juke-boxes in all Fatburger stores. They're loaded up with classic soul, R&B, and jazz, and people like to play it loud. The music is as big a part of the atmosphere as a Double King Burger.

For a truly diverse gift selection, hit Handmade Galleries. It's filled with an eclectic collection of one-of-a-kind items, and everything is fun *and* functional. See if they still have the Tingler in stock. It's like a copper claw, and you can shape it to fit your head. The manufacturers call it "the Ultimate Massager," and it's really unlike anything else. Have someone lower it onto your head, twist, raise it up, and repeat. It's the greatest goose-bumpy feeling! You'll also find scrapbooks, ceramics, vintage collections, furniture, ornate crafts, beautiful sake sets, and the Dirty Girl line of toiletries and bath additions.

For the music buff, there's Secondspin.com, which has both retail and online locations. Loads of used CDs, but you'd better set aside some time, 'cause it's so easy to get lost in the search for that first Dwight Twilley record. Maybe you can save this one for when you get home and do it online.

Carney's
12601 Ventura Boulevard, Studio City
(818) 761-8300
Psychic Eye Bookstore
13435 Ventura Boulevard, Sherman Oaks
(818) 906-8263
www.pebookstore.com
Vespa of California, Inc.
13629 Ventura Boulevard, Sherman Oaks
(818) 906-0350
Sherman Oaks Antique Mall
14034 Ventura Boulevard, Sherman Oaks
(818) 360-0338
Iguana Vintage Clothing
14422 Ventura Boulevard, Sherman Oaks
(818) 907-6716
Fatburger
14402 Ventura Boulevard, Sherman Oaks
(818) 905-3137
www.fatburger.com

Handmade Galleries
14556 Ventura Boulevard, Sherman Oaks
(818) 382-3444
Secondspin.com
14564 Ventura Boulevard, Sherman Oaks
(818) 986-6866

Where the High- and Lowbrow Meet for Coffee

Here's a conversation I had which perfectly describes the stretch of Vermont Boulevard betwixt Franklin and Sunset.

ME: I'm hungry.

FRIEND: Oh yeah?

ME: You want to get something to eat?

FRIEND: Sure. Where?

ME: We can walk to Vermont.

FRIEND: Where do you want to go?

ME: How about Fred 62's? It's cool.

FRIEND: Yeah, dude, like I really want to spend $6 on a grilled-cheese sandwich.

Yes, this little Los Feliz enclave—ostensibly an arty neighborhood strip—is not without its San Franciscoesque contradictions. One fine example is that the institutional alternative bookstore here, Amok, which, after years of providing leftist (and rightist) literature to neighborhood alternative-lifestylers, did finally fold. Meanwhile, the corner kiosk selling *People, Us, Teen,* and the like lives on. Archaic Idiot—a resale shop with vinyl, retro clothes, Keane prints, and a neat velvet painting of the devil taking a dump—still carries the anti-establishment stamp of approval; as does Mondo Video A-Go-Go, which rents out Russ Meyer films, Anton LaVey tapes, and tapes for every other fetish for that matter—inside, you can hear people say things like, "Those latte-drinking motherfuckers." Above and beyond the classic struggle between the proletariat and bourgeoisie, Vermont's charms are—how do you say?—real neat. Yes, the nouveau meatloaf at Fred's is expensive and, as they are everywhere else, so are the coffees at Figaro, a nice, tiled-floor retro 1920s French boulangerie. And the Dresden Room, featured in the movie Swingers, doesn't exactly have bebop-era prices. But who cares?—you're on vacation (and so have already chosen your side, you rich, college-educated snobs, you). While there, also take note of the little Japanese sushi/noodle shop, Mako Restaurant, with excellent, low-priced meals underneath the Los Feliz Theater awning; **Skylight Bookstore** (see chapter 3 listings); Y-QUE, which sells incense and a little bit of everything else; as well as Atmosphere, a strangely classy hybrid hawking fashionable clothing and . . . *hmmm* . . . novelty drug accessories.

Vermont Avenue, between Franklin Avenue and Sunset Boulevard

Archaic Idiot
1720 N. Vermont Avenue, Los Feliz
(323) 666-6354

Figaro Brasserie
1804 N. Vermont Avenue, Los Feliz
(323) 662-1587

Dresden Room
1760 N. Vermont Avenue, Los Feliz
(323) 665-4294

Mako Restaurant
1820 N. Vermont Avenue, Los Feliz
(323) 660-1211

Y-QUE
(323) 664-0021
www.yque.com

Atmosphere
1728 N. Vermont Avenue, Los Feliz
(323) 666-8420

CHAPTER 9

Places to Stay in Los Angeles

Shangri-la Behind Cement

The painted, cantinalike entrance of the Hotel Figueroa and the general business-district desolation on which it stands belie its inside beauty. With its gigantic ceilings, ornate tiles, and Santa Fe tapestries, the Figueroa resembles something between a Mexican City palace and the Hotel Pera in Turkey. An upstairs bar overlooking the lobby, as well as the one situated down a palatial hallway near where the pool and restaurant also sit, completes the effect, making this accommodation feel like a Shangri-la hidden behind sidewalks of concrete instead of the fabled waterfall. The Hotel Figueroa is perfect for business travelers seeking frills aplenty, or those who plan to visit the nearby Staples Center or the Convention Center.

Hotel Figueroa

939 South Figueroa Street, Los Angeles

(800) 421-9092

California Dreamin'

Ah, Los Angeles: blue skies, gorgeous mountain vistas, the beaches, the sun, the exorbitant price of real estate. Yes, people pay plenty for their houses on the hills here and, for that matter, their fixer-uppers in the sketchier parts of, say, Koreatown. Maybe that's why the sales agents here are so friendly when you visit their open houses. A favorite pastime of my ex-girlfriend's and mine was to spend a few fun hours on Sunday afternoons California dreamin'; that is, driving through various L.A. neighborhoods and popping into those houses with their FOR SALE signs out front. Posing as a young, married couple, we'd get a free look at beautiful and cramped houses going for astronomical prices. One such domicile was a pretty two-bedroomer with a loft, going for something like a trillion bucks. After we noticed out loud all the movie posters and photos of stars around the place, the agent informed us that the owner was a scriptwriter who was in the economic situation of having to downsize. *Poor guy*, we mused. *Guess he'll never get his house in the hills.* Sure, such an activity can be disheartening for all parties involved, but if you're one of those folks who have come here thinking about resettling, doing what we did might be a real eye-opener; and afterward, suddenly your ten-bedroom Victorian in Ohio, which you got for the low, low price of $100,000, may not seem so bad anymore.

House Shopping in Los Angeles
All-inclusive

Where to Sleep When You Are Homeless
Being homeless is less imprisoning than living with a mortgage, a car payment, insurance, and 2.3 sniveling, money-hoarding brats. The American dream is too simple and unsatisfying, we think. In fact, one can become quite comfortable on the streets, if one only knows where to sleep. Naturally, the more beautiful places in the city proper, the ones with lush greenery and plenty of space, belong to Beverly Hills and the Hollywood Hills, where people are not so tolerant of vagabond activity. Screw those snobs;

they're serving a life sentence to the ego, and we're egoless, right? Go to Topanga Canyon, between Woodland Hills and Malibu. It is an expansive area with plenty of nature and woodsy/artsy/crafty types selling precious stones, dream-catchers, and stuff. It gets cold at night, and frogs, raccoons, skunks, and possums will share your sleeping quarters, but hey—*company!* Besides, bus benches are bad for the back, and general sidewalks attract foot traffic, some of which attract workforce nuts. *Gross!* Topanga Canyon is a thousand miles from activity, and will force your hand at survival—but that is what being free is all about!

Topanga Canyon
Take 101 north to Topanga Canyon Boulevard, and head west. The woods are a couple of miles up.

Keeping It on the Lowdown
A veritable "retropolis" with all the throwback and individualized style that you yourself can appreciate, that is the Safari Inn. It is a Burbank landmark, and as low-key as some motor inn from the movie pictures (namely, *True Romance*, a Quentin Tarantino film that made the Safari a villain versus villain cultlike must see), only this is tropical, with tiki spears and bamboo and lots of palms. And it has been freshly renovated, giving it the modernity of any downtown Hyatt and the stylishness of any . . . downtown Hyatt. Only with tiki stuff and palms. It do have class. Relax by the pool with an iced tea or some other delight from room service, or recline on the sundeck and soak in the SoCal sunshine, whispering sweet nothings to your companion. The Safari is a perfect place to let all anxiety and pressure slip off your back. Everything is easygoing. Each of the fifty-five rooms has a mini-refrigerator for those cold Silver Bullets, as well as HBO (seems a given, really, but nobody wants to miss reruns of *Mr. Show*). And hey, ironing boards! No need to look shabby. The Olive Bistro & Lounge serves up breakfast, lunch, and dinner,

offering a unique menu with traditional and innovative cuisine. The Inn is located in relative proximity to NBC studios, the Media Center Mall, and Dimples karaoke bar, where stars are being born even as this is being written. Golly, Burbank is a hive of entertainment and fun.

Safari Inn
1911 West Olive Avenue, Burbank
(818) 845-0054
Reservations: (800) 782-4373

Luxury Lodged in the Windpipes of Studio City

If you are looking for a quiet place to stay that is removed from the frantic buzz of Hollywood yet still within a stone's throw, check out The Sportsman's Lodge in Studio City. Centrally located near Universal and Warner Bros. Studios, as well as a thousand unique shops along Ventura Boulevard, it could be the perfect place to stay (affordably) in vicinity. Eight acres of heavily manicured yet rustic land make up the premises, along with 177 guest rooms, nineteenth-century Georgia- or Country-style (many of which have a pool view), as well as 13 executive suites that are suited for kings (and queens). Speaking of the pool, we are talking a heated, Olympic-sized, always clean with the right amount of chlorine kind of pool, with a lot of bronzed gods and fit lionesses along the perimeter. Just like you see in the late-night cable movies. Bikinis, Speedos, thongs, stumbling cabana boy with his stilted fingers balancing a tray, nearly dropping it due to the distractions, get the idea? The Jacuzzi is a good place to dip the toes after a swim. The Sportsman's Lodge also has meeting and banquet facilities, an exercise room, the Muddy Moose bar & grill, the Pub (*Resident Tourist*'s favorite hang), and the Patio Café, with all the meatloaf, country-fried steak, and egg-white omelets you can manage. Belch. Courtesy shuttle vans will get you to and from the Burbank airport, Universal

Studios, or anywhere. Just ask. And don't think that celebrities are not spotted here, either. There is always a check-me-out silver-screener nearby.

The Sportsman's Lodge
12825 Ventura Boulevard, Studio City
(818) 769-4700 or (800) 821-8511
Or E-mail: information@slhotel.com

The USA Hostel on Schrader . . . Oh, the Depraved Memories

By six-thirty we were stuffed and well on our way to being drunk. Five-dollar all-you-can-eat burgers and dogs and $1 cans of beer, after all, are the best prices in Hollywood. We—my date and I—had talked our way (I was from Michigan, she from New York; we met on a train) into the USA Hostel on Schrader, a comely violet little house made only for out-of-towners with a penchant for adventure. When I turned my back to get another round, a young Frenchman wearing jeans that had the Looney Tune and Disney characters hand-painted on them, began hitting on my date, apparently telling her that he didn't know Asian women could be so tall. Her eyebrow raised with perturbation as she drunkenly relayed the story back to me later. By ten P.M. we were mingling in the upstairs bar and some friends we had smuggled in were tackling the Foosball table. Another had become so drunk, the powers that be told him he had to scram; he did, taking the gamers with him, as foreigners madly downed libations and swayed to the watered-down sounds of American popular tunes ("Everybody Dance Now"). Then, a nice crooner with a guitar took the stage and played some Oasis tunes. (On Sunday nights, stand-ups provide the entertainment and, according to the management, give the best comedy relief in all of L.A.) This wayward musician asked me to join him (I admitted I could strum a few chords) and I agreed, but my show time never materialized, as my date and I stumbled out of the hostel and onto Hollywood Boulevard, where we had a drink at the newly renovated Pig 'N Whistle next to the recently refurbished Egyptian Theater. When we came back, some devious little devils had left notes on the table instructing everyone to go to our room for an orgy. Wastedly, I leaned in and told the lobby girl: "Hey, did you know there's an orgy in room 212?" "I only go for one person at a time," she answered. "It's just a joke," I replied and walked with my date to our room, where we passed out . . . alone! That is, just the two of us. The next morning, hung over, I noticed all the fun events this little hostel had on its agenda (cross-dressing parties, pimps-and-ho's gatherings) and vowed to come back someday—or, should they catch on to my little game, try one of the many other hostels in the city.

Hollywood Youth Hostel, USA Hostel
1624 Schrader, Los Angeles
(323)462-3777
Additional hostel locations:
Banana Bungalow
2775 Cahuenga Boulevard, Hollywood
(323) 851-1129
Orange Drive Manor
1764 N. Orange Drive, Hollywood
(323) 850-0350
Orbit Hotel
7950 Melrose Avenue, West Hollywood
(323) 655-1510
Student Inn
7083½ Hollywood Boulevard, Hollywood
(323) 469-6781
HI (Hosteling International)–Los Angeles/Santa Monica Hostel
1435 Second Street, Santa Monica
(310) 393-9913

Why Visit When You Can Stay?

By now you have seen that Los Angeles has umpteen million things to do, and your wild spirit wants to return as soon as possible to take up residence here. Oklahoma has never seemed so boring, and you are sick to death of fried dough, moonshine, and that perpetual case of skitters. Get out of there! We won't dissuade you from coming to Los Angeles; we like your kind. So stop dicking around, eh? Your first visit should be Westside Rentals, a comprehensive apartment/town home/house locator. Westside Rentals will provide you with a service that none of your friends already living in Los Angeles can. They will find that beach shack in Manhattan for you to set up a drug cartel, or that suave studio in Hollywood to hang your artwork in, or even that duplex you have been craving in Covina. They will find you what you're looking for, in short. There are six Westside Rentals locations in southern California (listed later), and the $60 membership fee is good for sixty days. It is an ideal setup if you are making a long-distance move. Remember: If you find a place quickly, you can give your friend the password and let them find a place to live, too. (Keep your mouth shut about that, or else!) It is beneficial all the way around. There are over 10,000 listings at Westside Rentals, so there must be at least a couple located exactly where you are looking. Your time is saved for the affordable bar tab of $60—and that isn't bad. (If you are really looking to live in Covina, you are not really leaving Oklahoma, now, are you, Mr. Joad?) Check out www.westsiderentals.com for more information.

Westside Rentals
Melrose: 7213 Melrose Avenue, #B, Hollywood
(323) 634-RENT
The Valley: 12516 Ventura Boulevard, Studio City
(818) 623-4444
South Bay: 524 Pacific Coast Highway, Hermosa Beach
(310) 372-RENT

West Side: 1110 Wilshire Boulevard, Santa Monica
(310) 395-RENT
Pasadena: 130 N. Fair Oaks Avenue, Pasadena
(626) 798-RENT
Orange County: 19475 Beach Boulevard, Huntington Beach
(714) 840-RENT

CHAPTER 10

Shopping in Los Angeles

Hey, What's Your Bag?

It's inevitable. You will shop. So the best thing we can do is lead you toward places with more flavor, with more imagination, in most of which you'll actually spend less money. We're dragons for a bargain and aim to keep you away from a mall, if it's within our power. It's a journey, this L.A. shopping thing, so be prepared. Eyes peeled, wallets prepped.

Eritrea + Djibouti + Oklahoma = Diabolical Fun!

The California Map and Travel store is a universal resource for *anybody* thinking of going *anywhere*, including Mars! That is overly ambitious for a place whose motto is "We Carry the World!" They carry our celestial neighbors as well. But seriously: It is an essential stop if you are planning a business or leisure trip

151

to Africa, Australia, Montreal, Katmandu, or Easter Island—or even Bakersfield—because they have guides! There are over 20,000 titles of atlases, maps, language books, cultural books, topographical maps, food and drink texts, religious tomes, travel narratives, erotic travel tips and tales, and just about anything that deals with travel interest. Just browsing? Check out the assortment of state/country flags, accessories such as travel games, eye shades, neck pillows, electrical converters, calenders, travel journals, money belts, earplugs, and other such jet-lagging zigzag. Or go to the fingertouch TOPO map machine, where you can dwindle down the United States into a bucolic cul-de-sac in Broomfield, thus feeling large in the process. There is something amazing about the selection of globes, too. They come in all kinds of different colors, shapes, sizes, and worldly dimensions. Cold? Check out the squeaking fire in the back. (Shh, it's not real.) It's perfect to read about the nearly forgotten kingdom of East Prussia by the cool fire.

California Map and Travel
3312 Pico Boulevard, Santa Monica
(310) 396-6277

Alice & Annie's
This one is an absolute hidden treasure of Los Angeles proper. It's got gorgeous vintage clothes, at prices that are about one-third of what they're charging in pricey boutiques over the hill. Breathtaking suits, ravishing rayon dresses from the 1940s, sheer blouses—I could drop a pile of money with each visit. It's exactly the same stuff you find at the more expensive places, too. And for that special occasion, check out the formal wear. In fact, this was the first stop on a recent shopping expedition to find the perfect maid-of-honor dress. Everything is in mint, albeit vintage, condition, including the accessories.

Alice & Annie's
11056 Magnolia Boulevard, North Hollywood
(818) 761-6085

So You Think You're in the "Need to Know," Do You?

You *really* want to go shopping? Forget the malls. This is the real, real deal. Thousands of choices and no retail prices in sight. The Alley has to be your first stop. Merchants are jammed into this block, offering everything you could imagine, at unimaginable prices. How about a genuine leather bag for $6? That's just the beginning. Clothes and shoes for the entire family, accessories, cosmetics, toiletries . . . it's all here. And you've got the entire Fashion District for your browsing pleasure. It's nearly overwhelming, these nearly fifty city blocks of stuff. It's a mix of retail and wholesale, so be aware.

The Alley at Santee Street
Between Olympic and 12th Street, and Santee and Maple, Downtown

Triumvirate of Beauty and the Beautiful Woman Who Emerged

Just cause you're on vacation doesn't mean you won't need a new Scrunchy, or new hair color for that matter. For color and accessories, check out Ball Beauty on Fairfax or Sterling Beauty on Vine. They're both in the middle, or really close to other spots mentioned in this book, so they're right on your way to somewhere. Ball Beauty is across the street from **Canter's Deli**, so after you pick up your Krazy Color in Aubergine, Capri Blue, or Poppy Red, head over for a knish. Sterling is big, and has a huge selection of every conceivable hair color and brand, as well as brushes, hairpins, and scarves. Manicure and pedicure products, too, for the well-groomed you. Then again, it's really cool to come home with a new 'do. Now, you might be tempted to visit some swanky salon in Beverly Hills, but save the money. Fantastic Sam's at the corner of Sunset and La Brea might look like just another cheap haircut chain, but don't be put off. The price is right ($13.95) for your normal cut and shampoo, and the stylists know what they're doing. Highly recommended are Keiko and Cherie. Call first, to see if they're there. They both give really great, fast cuts, and Keiko is a real pistol.

Ball Beauty
416 N. Fairfax Avenue, Los Angeles
(323) 655-2330
Sterling Beauty
1244 Vine Street, Los Angeles
(323) 463-6801
Fantastic Sam's
7111 Sunset Boulevard, Los Angeles
(323) 850-1770 or (323) 272-SAMS

Medical Needs and Love Charms, One-Stop Shopping

The Botica Million Dollar is a sociology experiment in action. Nestled on the corner of Broadway and Third, downtown (and right across the street from the Bradbury Building), it reflects both the modernism and the superstition of Latino culture. Bottles of aspirin, cans of hairspray, colognes, and soaps for your secular needs sit on shelves nearby other rows that carry items designed to capture all your spiritual desires. Looking for love? Wealth? A long life? Well, don't bother with the pharmacist situated in the back of the store—no. Instead, buy a votive candle to light, some incense to burn, or purchase some blessed soap instead. Or go to the front counter, where the clerk will help you pick out the most useful statue of a saint or angel—you know, something to go next to your dream-catcher or wind chimes at home. If you're hungover, however, well, then never mind that stuff. We suggest a couple of Extra-Strength Excedrin or a bowl of menudo, which can be purchased at the Grand Central Market or many of the various restaurants on Broadway. And if you're experiencing prolonged pain or have come down with strange itching scabs anywhere on, or inside your body—by all means consult your physician!

Botica Million Dollar
301 S. Broadway, Los Angeles
(213) 687-3688

Bad Neighborhood Spells Fat Pickings
This one's not in a cool section of town, which probably explains why it's not picked through. It's tucked just past the Kaiser Permanente complex, right across from Children's Hospital, hence the name. It's not quite Los Feliz, and it's east of Hollywood, so it's sort of a no-man's-land. But the selection is great. Lots of wonderful glassware, toys, books, and I found the most amazing dress for my daughter here when she was small. It was handmade, cotton print in red, green, and yellow, with sweet, sweet yellow rickrack edging the neck and hem. It's exactly something my mom would have made for me, as she made most of our clothes, and I loved it. And it was $1!

Children's Hospital Thrift Shop
4551 W. Sunset Boulevard, Los Angeles
(323) 663-1975

Men without Hats Were Inspired by a Little Store on Centinela Avenue
The Northridge earthquake of 1994 left millions of people dead and/or worried about safety. Living in southern California has a rather peculiar asterisk attached to it, which says: "You are on a major fault line. Any day now could be your last." Don't take that poppycock lying down—fight back! Shop at Family First, a babyproofing and earthquake safety merchandiser, to ensure you are taking the right measures against the underlying Big One. Check this out: You can purchase furniture straps, mirror safety

hooks, first-aid kits, flashlights, emergency survival supplies (a brick of dry compact food, water, a blanket, and light), solar rechargeable lanterns, power-failure nightlights, television safety brackets, quake hold museum putty, and tons of other precautionary equipment. Family First is mostly a child-safety place, though, and sells a great many devices to keep little "agoo" out of harm's way. Things like the padded potty seat and corner kushions [sic] are designed to soften those staggering head-blows that normally have toddlers concussing, thus causing adults' irresponsible hearts to break. You probably will have trouble trying to stop tectonic plates from shifting. That's understandable, mortal tourist, you're not the Almighty. (So stop acting like you are!) Get safe at Family First.

Family First
3523 Centinela Avenue, Los Angeles
(310) 390-0210 or (800) 41-STEPS
www.familyfirstonline.com

"Mommy, Look . . . I Made a Poopy."

A treasure trove of toddlers' clothes is Flapjack. All used but, considering how long they wear them before they grow out of them, not by much. Sizes range from newborn to age 10 or so, with such a fine selection and great quality, you might not have to shop anywhere else. You'll have the best-dressed baby in town, for a fraction of the price. They also carry shoes, toys, books, baby furniture, and paraphernalia, and will often take your gently used clothes and things in trade, or pay you cash, but always call first.

Flapjack
10590 Pico Boulevard, West Los Angeles
(310) 204-1896

Wake Up and Smell the Roses

Los Angeles, especially downtown, has a certain beauty just before the sun comes up. And one place to experience that is the

Flower District, as it gets moving early, in the predawn hours. For non-trade people (us regular folk) it opens at 6 A.M., Tuesday, Thursday, and Saturday. Monday, Wednesday, and Friday, it's 8 A.M. For the trade, things get going at 2 A.M. One loses count of the varieties of blooms available. The hues and scents are overwhelming and the selection equally so. Greens, blues, purples, fuchsias— the wild colors are jolting in their intensities. Whether it's the delicate Queen Anne's lace or the substantially succulent donkey-tail, or even artichokes on the stem, if you're in the market for foliage, you'll not go home empty-handed. And also find any and all accoutrements to complete the picture. Vases, pots, Styrofoam bases, bridal wreath collars—whatever you need, check out Moskatel's, right next door. It's a vast arts, crafts, and decorating emporium. Need Styrofoam balls of varying sizes for that Solar System model project? Here they are. Disco-ball holiday ornaments? Here, too. Want to make some unique soap? Molds, dyes, and soap itself, right here. Holiday headquarters indeed. Parking is convenient, as well; either on the street at meters, or at the parking structure, 742 Wall Street.

Flower District
755 Wall Street, Los Angeles
www.laflowerdistrict.com
Moskatel's
738 Wall Street, Los Angeles

Secondhand Rounding Third

I've been to a lot of Goodwill Stores, and this one is my favorite. It's so organized, largely by color within each separate section, and while the quality of the merchandise is high, it is remarkably low priced. On my last trip in, I found a pair of cargo shorts, nearly new, but nicely broken in, for $2.99; a never-worn pair of women's Keds for $3.99; an almost-new pair of what looked to be a really expensive pair of women's leather dress shoes for $3.99; and a beautiful green-striped, softly worn Gap T-shirt for 99 cents! They've got new mattresses for $125 apiece, furniture, and a great selection of kids' clothes.

Goodwill
200 Vine Street, Hollywood
(323) 469-2357

I Like the Baked Coconut

The only thing I can say about the Grand Central Market—a bustling affair established in 1917 with numerous produce-sellers, a strong variety of restaurants, cafés, and dried goods and meat dealers—that probably hasn't been said before is this: You've got to try the baked coconut there. It's a delicious and sugary treat. The end. Oh, a couple more things: The Market is open all week from 9 A.M. to 6 P.M., and it's a great place for people-watching.

Grand Central Market
317 S. Broadway, Downtown
(213) 624-2378
For more information, go to www.grandcentralsquare.com

Tambourine Player Wanted

We try to sway people from two things: (1) buying those chintzy maps to the stars' homes; and (2) trying to make it big in a rock band in Los Angeles. If you're bound and determined to go about breaking rule number one, well, there's nothing much we can say. But if, on the other hand, you're dead-set on continuing on a no-compromise road to rock-and-roll fame, or oblivion, as it were, in L.A., might we suggest the Guitar Center on Sunset Boulevard? And not for its Rock Walk, which features the handprints of such big-name acts as Aerosmith and KISS, outside its big doors, nor for its overwhelmingly massive selection of all kinds of instruments—no. Instead, we've got something a little more basic in mind. When you walk into this huge national (this one is the original) chain store's entrance, at first, try to ignore the inclination to put a $5,000 classic Fender on your credit card. Instead go directly to the little office on the right, which features, on one wall, a handy-dandy corkboard; on it, a whole slew of tacked-up notices from other poor musician types looking for all kinds of players (guitarists, drummers, flautists, etc.). Write down—did we tell you to be sure to bring a pen?—the numbers attached to your favorite listings (or tack a note up yourself, should you still have the urge to rock, swing, beat-box, spin). Then proceed directly home, grow your hair just right, learn your scales, and, once this is all done, throw on your best egotistical genius musician air and make the phone call, dude.

Guitar Center
7425 Sunset Boulevard, Los Angeles
(323) 874-1060

People in Black Buy Basil

There are many, many farmers' markets throughout the city, and through the week. Some are smaller, neighborhood deals, but this is not one of them. The Hollywood Farmers' Market, held each Sunday morning, stretches for blocks, and features not only the organic produce one normally finds at a farmers' market, but fresh fish, bread, crafts, and more. It's also *the* place for a lot of the night crawlers devoted to the Hollywood scene to be, bright and early Sunday morning. It's popular and hip, and sometimes you get the feeling you never left the club on Saturday night. There is a wide choice of produce, samples of which are sometimes given out. There's a guy selling fresh herbs whose black lab lazily watches over the goods. Tamales are also a popular purchase and the line is long, but the wait is worth it.

Hollywood Farmers' Market
Ivar, between Sunset and Hollywood Boulevards
Every Sunday morning

Cheap-Ass Souvenirs

Okay, so Hollywood T-shirts isn't exactly off the beaten path, but go to hell, neither are you! As far as cheesy, tourist-friendly gag gifts and gewgaws go, this place is a sucker trap like all the others in the nearby vicinity, make no qualms about it. However, shoppers of Hollywood T-shirts will get something that may not be elsewhere, a sense of fulfillment. In a word: quantity! Wasn't it Oscar Wilde who said, "Nowadays we know the price of everything, but the value of nothing"? Holy Moses, he must have a purgatory station over Hollywood Boulevard! You can get *five* T-shirts for $10! That is not a misprint, *five* T-shirts for ten American doll-hairs, take-home price, wholesale, dirt-cheap, unbeatable! Plus tax. And these shirts are anti-fashionable, and cursedly poor in taste, more than anything you could find on Melrose Avenue, capturing the very essence of Los Angeles. They have aphorisms and maxims that are bound to befuddle the most stringent clerisy back home in Beaumont, Texas. They say ridiculous things in pink and yellow pastels like I'M THE BOSS, WAY COOL, or CALIFORNIA. Ridiculous, but perfect for a throw rag to check the oil on your rig back home. They also sell magnets, mugs, celebrity pictures, and other cheap-ass memorabilia.

Hollywood T-shirts
6735 Hollywood Boulevard, Hollywood
(323) 469-4683

Jewelry That Makes People Say: "How Pulchritudinous!"

Los Feliz is a quiet, well-to-do area of Los Angeles, whose artistry is most evident in its storefronts and restaurants. Everything smells of orange blossom and macadamia nuts and green olives, and the occasional blast of anise. Next time you are taking your special little minx out that way, swing by LS on Hillhurst Avenue, a jewelry shop with all the earthy bracelets, rings, and necklaces one could ever hope for. Gentlemen, she will love you

160

if you do. Russian-born owner Liza Shtromberg designs rock pieces that sing to the primitive animal within us. Her jewelry garments also bring much needed fierceness to celebrity types, like world-renowned director Stan Bolinowitz, who regularly frequents the shop and can be seen wearing Liza's chandelier earrings most of the time. Ms. Shtromberg uses anything from freshwater pearls to Peruvian opals to citrine and other precious stones in creating her famous masterpieces, along with plenty of sterling silver. The store itself is esoteric but unassuming. It is small and vaguely minimalist, but still rich with plenty of handmade pieces that are perfect for gifts, wardrobe accessorizing, or decadent subtlety for your own use. Liza is on premises often, and will be happy to break down the difference between sapphires and amethysts if you are color-blind.

LS
2120 N. Hillhurst Avenue, Los Feliz
(323) 913-1444

An Heiress's Undergarments

A young socialite bought a pair of custom underpants that a friend of mine made by ironing onto them a printout of a $100 bill. The socialite was dating a well-known young actor at the time, so my friend mused on whether or not he ever took them off of her . . . with his teeth. My story was much less sexy (though equally L.A.): I picked up a wheatgrass plant for $10, took it home, and put it on my balcony. Occasionally I'd snip the plants tips and add the blades to my morning drinks; until, of course, the plant died. (By then, my health kick had pretty much run its course anyway.) Yes, the Melrose Trading Post, on the corner of Melrose and Fairfax, is a good way to spend a Sunday morning or afternoon spending. Vintage clothes and used CDs and old movie posters and all kinds of antiques and junk are what you'll find here in up to 160 booths that open up at 7:00 A.M. Admission, paid outside the gated parking lot of Fairfax High School, is $2 for adults and goes toward buying computers and the like for the students who run it, along with faculty and staff.

Melrose Trading Post
At Fairfax High School, 7850 Melrose Avenue, Los Angeles
For more information, call (323) 655-POST

Pinch Your Pennies with All Your Might!

Every state must have its own version of this, but SoCal's 99-Cents-Only Store certainly must be the grande dame. I have friends who say they just couldn't bring themselves to go in, and they're not just crazy, they're missing out! The first store opened in 1982 on La Tijera Boulevard, and since then they've just exploded. It's *the* place for any cleansers or toiletries. I've found Freeman Botanical Leave-In Conditioner/Detangling Spray here, which elsewhere sells for much more. Any shampoo you can find in a grocery or drugstore, it's almost guaranteed you'll save serious money here. Deodorant, toothpaste, brushes, cotton swabs—you buy them anywhere else, it's insanity. Dish soap, laundry detergent, pine cleanser, brooms, mops . . . same deal. And now they also have refrigerated sections, where you can find eggs at a dozen for 99 cents. Occasionally a dozen eggs are on sale at the grocery superstore for $1.99. *Hmmm.* Bacon has shown up, perfectly fry-able, sour cream, frozen lemonade. As well, take a stroll by the "bakery": English muffins, bagels, corn muffins (the really big, sweet kind), bread, tortillas—I'm telling you, a trip once a week is *essential.* I could just go on and on. Pasta, graham crackers, sodas, bottled water, baby wipes, moisturizer, refried beans, applesauce, shaving cream—check here first! They've even started carrying beer and wine, and it's perfectly potable, thank you very much. The stores are kept in wonderful order, and are well lit and clean. They're well known for their colorfully coordinated window displays and store organization. They'll do kooky things, like when a new store opens, the first ninety-nine people get a TV or a microwave. And for seasonal stuff, this is the only place you need to know about. Pastel Easter eggs, spiderwebs for Halloween, any kind of Santa Claus or menorah you might desire—they're all here, in multiple shapes and sizes. For the tourist, it's really the only place to run in and get that toothbrush or those sunglasses you forgot, or snacks and water for the car. It's a gold mine, simply put.

99-Cents-Only Stores
Various locations
(800) LUCKY-99

All the Pretty Junk

If you've forgotten how beautiful U.S.-made junk can be, you might want to pop your head into this pretty little shop. Established in 1979 and at its current digs on Melrose Avenue since 1981, Off the Wall—Antiques & Weird Stuff is chock-full of only the best in Americana; and priced appropriately. (It's not like you'll even be able to get half of this stuff on the plane back home anyway, so don't fret about your meager pocketbook.) A gorgeous Art Deco bar with circular mirrors lines one wall, while an oversized replica of the Millennium Falcon (one of only fifty issued by Toys-Я-Us) flies above, with a dangling price tag of $2,800. Up there, too, is the Jolly Green Giant, in mint condition behind his plastic covering. There's more, too: wooden—the old kind—pinball machines and figurines; classic framed posters (a 3-D picture of something called *Phantom of the Rue Morgue*), dolls, and a white Deco panther for your fireplace room floor. All of it, whether culled from a dead star's home or from the set of a B-movie, is strangely classy-looking. Even the Plexiglas Ronald McDonald (there at time of publication), the king of American schlock, somehow looks regal as he waves good-bye to you on your way out.

Off the Wall—Antiques & Weird Stuff
7325 Melrose Avenue, Los Angeles
(323) 930-1185

Come for the Music, Stay for the Memories

Rockaway Records, a shrine to that greatest of perfected American art forms, rock and roll, is at first look just your average record outlet—but then, it's really not average at all. Owners and brothers Gary and Wayne Johnson have, besides seeing fit to shirk the common rules of distributorship (good for them) by keeping a well-stocked local music section, have also made it their business to maintain a thoroughly versed compendium of music memorabilia; and you gotta love 'em for it. Nestled in the back of Rockaway is an ever-changing lineup of old, unused concert tickets; ancient teenybopper magazines featuring your favorite musicians; collectible records; even a couple of copies of the version—no bloody babies—of the Beatles' "Butcher Block" album (actually titled *Yesterday & Today*) and a goodly amount of Elvis vinyl; original lyric sheets; old backstage passes to concerts featuring such mega–rock gods as KISS; music-related toys (the plastic Elvis guitar is cute); as well as many other interesting and surprising nook-and-cranny rock memories, all for sale at prices ranging from pretty low, to "Damn, wow—I can't ever afford that" expensive. There's also a plastic stage pass for one Yanni tour priced at $3; please feel free to buy it—'cause we're not gonna do it!

Rockaway Records
2395 Glendale Boulevard, Los Angeles
(323) 664-3232

Ladies and Gentlemen, Introducing the Fabulous Flyswatter

As far as Farmers' Markets go, the Silver Lake one is pretty negligible (and, for your entertainment money, you might do better with the more high-profile one at Fairfax and Third); still, we like the Sunset Junction aesthetic with its last bastion of bohemian sensibilities, its fun folk artiness. So, if you think of the Market here as a weighing point to bigger and better things (fun cafés, resale shops, and cool knickknack and clothing stores right down the street), then this one (open for biz on Saturdays) might be more worth your time. Plus, as far as we know, the one at Fairfax doesn't have the guy who sells ladybug farms in plastic toy-dispenser containers and the not-so-world-famous mosquito bat from Thailand, which, for $12, comes with batteries and acts as an electric zapper on those pesky household pests as well as unwanted beer-swilling neighbors. "Ouch, what did you do that for?" you can almost hear someone say, as you hold the red plastic tennis racquet–like apparatus in your hand and swat the air. Good times, folks. Good times.

Silver Lake Farmers' Market
At Sunset Junction
3700 Sunset Boulevard, Los Angeles

Finally!

You know how hard is it to get a copy of the *Tiki Times* around this town? After searching high and low for years, I was just about at my wits' end until I popped into Soap Plant Wacko on one brisk Saturday afternoon. There, right on the counter, was the latest issue staring me right in the face. Imagine my elated surprise! Even better, they had those candy buttons I used to eat as a child. You know the ones—the little cloying dots of colored sugar on the rectangular pieces of white paper. With Alice Cooper suffusing my ears, I moved farther into this giant store, past the makeup section (I made a mental note to get the virgin/slut lip balm for my next girlfriend), past the art books, the postcards, the Bruce Lee action figure. The Bruce Lee Action Figure! What?! I stopped. They have this, too. Awesome! Totally awesome! And there, too, were all the members of Metallica cast in plastic; a renegade cutoff foot sitting in a box of mishmash; a whole wall of metal wind-up toys; a blow-up palm tree that would look perfect next to my bar at home; and the crown prince of them all: a plastic Frankenstein with a gigantic head and a hefty price tag to match. In the back, I took a look around the La Luz de Jesus Gallery, which features month-long exhibits of artists with the apparent same taste in modern pop-culture cartoonica as the rest of Soap Plant Wacko: folks like "The Pizz," whose painting of a bunch of hillbillies with a twister in the background pleased well; and Neon Park, who did the cover art for the Mothers of Invention's *Weasels Ripped My Flesh* album. There were others like Gary Taxali and Gin Stevens, as well as Krystine Kryttre. As I made my way out of the building, I passed a box of Kewpie-doll heads and decided that this was the place for me—oh, I'd be back all right.

Soap Plant Wacko
4633 Hollywood Boulevard, Los Angeles
(323) 663-0122
La Luz de Jesus Gallery
4633 Hollywood Boulevard, Los Angeles
(323) 666-7667

Penny Whistles, Kazoos, Violins, and Guitar Picks

It takes fifty years to build the kind of reputation that Stein on Vine has, which is one of multidimensional quality. Imagine the difficulty in catering to those finicky musician types who need everything brought to them precisely, or else: "Boohoo!" The big babies! At least the bulk of who comes through Stein on Vine are jazz- and classical-minded musicians, instead of the standard Hollywood rock icon with his head up his toot. Nevertheless, they cater indiscriminately to all. At the entrance to this very quaint, non-intimidating ministore, there is a board to peruse for bands looking for specific members, specific members looking for bands, music lessons, equipment sales, etc., which is helpful for music-minded people unfamiliar with the area. SOV also does repairs and studio rentals, and has a place for band rehearsals (inquire within). Signed pictures of jazz greatness align the walls, and every instrument under the sun can be found (or ordered) here, a great resource for theater companies that need the sound effects. Egg shakers, didgeridoos, finger cymbals, the triangle, castanets, clarinets, saxophones, megaphones, cell phones (bullshit)—

anything! Get your guitar or violin strings, wahwah pedals, wood-wind and jazz theory books, songbooks, guitar polish (you flying-V bastards with the spandex know about that), penny whistles, tambourines, spoons, and whatnot from genuine people. Say hello to Gary Chen-Stein, or Maury Stein (the owner), and tell them *Resident Tourist* sent you. And if you want lessons on a given instrument, ask them. They will happily give you a referral.

Stein on Vine
848 Vine Street, Hollywood
(323) 467-7341

Swap-Meet Circuit

Four swap-meets on a regular monthly schedule take turns to show off terrific slices of L.A. life. You'll see celebrities, serious collectors, trend-followers, and just regular folks inspecting all the wares offered by hundreds of vendors. Some of these have new merchandise mixed in, and some are strictly antiques and collectibles. The Rose Bowl is reportedly the biggest of its kind in the country. You'll wander endlessly through rows and rows of metal lunchboxes, racks of clothing, furniture, toys, telephones, Bauer pottery, Bakelite bracelets—it practically goes on forever. Pasadena City College has a renowned record section, for all the visiting vinyl junkies. They all get started early, and some have early-bird entrance fees, for those who wanted to get started even earlier.

Rose Bowl
Second Sunday of every month
Near Highway 110 and Colorado Boulevard, Pasadena
(323) 560-SHOW
Pasadena City College
First Sunday of every month
1570 E. Colorado Boulevard, Pasadena
(626) 584-7906
Long Beach Outdoor Antique Market
Third Sunday of every month

Veteran's Stadium, Long Beach
Lakewood Boulevard and Covenant Street
Santa Monica Antiques and Collectibles
Fourth Sunday of every month
Santa Monica Airport

Organic Pork and Dried Goods

Trader Joe's is predominantly a southern California phenomenon. Stores have appeared in other parts of the country, but it's predominantly S.C. born and bred. The ripple of excitement that goes through a neighborhood when a Trader Joe's goes up is palpable. It's a grocery store of sorts, but the prices, quality, and selection have made it much more than that. Leave the hotel minibar locked up and head to TJ's to stock up on beer, wine, other beverages, snacks, and veggies. Heck, if you have a kitchenette, you're set, as they have a great refrigerated/frozen section, too. The wine selection alone makes it worth a trip. You'll have hundreds of choices of wines from all over the world, and many are priced below $6.99 a bottle. Trader Joe's own label wines are uniformly delicious, and more than reasonably priced. Beers such as Fat Weasel Pale Ale are also priced to accommodate. Cheeses, cold cuts, fruit, breads . . . Here's the place to go for picnic lunches for the beach. As well, take a look at the vitamins, pastas, and toiletries. People who are regular visitors to L.A. know to make Trader Joe's one of their first stops upon arriving.

Trader Joe's
Various locations
1-800-SHOP-TJS
www.traderjoes.com

Building a Fence at the Expense of Tyranny

Virgil's Hardware is a seventy-five-year-old family-owned stalwart for Mr. Fix-It, surviving the globalization of all the immense hardware stores that have overtaken Los Angeles, and the rest of the country. I mean, Ma and Pa come here and shop for lawn and gardening trinkets in the nursery, while enjoying home-made pickles at the checkouts, whistling Dixie in the aisles, and chatting about old man Johnson who lives down the road. It has the feel of a time when things weren't so frantically paced. Customer service at Virgil's is tops, too. Specialists are placed at stations and they shyly ask you ever so often, "Can I help you with anything?" See there? They're looking to help out in any way possible. Those residents and tourists who want to support hard-working family businesses instead of giving in to despotic corporate overthrow companies would love Virgil's on principle alone. It is a first-name company, where they get to know you. And hey, they carry the same wheelbarrows, toilet seats, plumbing, electrical, and automotive supplies as Home Depot. And seriously, try the pickles.

Virgil's Hardware
520 N. Glendale Avenue, Glendale
(818) 242-1104

Oh, the Irony!
All the cute little toys—which include wind-up walking brains, noses, ears, and mice (they apparently forgot the mice with ears growing out of their backs, as recently created by bioscientists); plastic nuns shooting sparks; the Jesus action figure, as well as pooping barn animals and various other tin and wooden collectibles—apparently don't bring a smile to the face of the curmudgeonly, graying old man, Mr. St. Michael, behind the counter anymore. When informed that we wanted to include his store in our book, the first thing he gruffly asked was: "How much is it going to cost?" "Nothing, not a thing," we answered. Mr. St. Michael went on to give his son, Jody, full credit for the store, which was founded all the way back in 1983. He then proceeded to get so riled up that he suggested we leave because we looked suspicious, taking our notes. We assured him we weren't writing

down prices, but he was undaunted. Don't let this be a deterrent! Despite the bizarre management style employed here, the Wound & Wound Toy Co. is a wondrous little Santa's workshop. (Could Mr. St. Michael actually be old Saint Nick? We're pretty sure that we, too, would get a little teed-off, having to keep lazy elves from sloughing off on such a tight schedule.) For kids of all ages, as well as grabby collectors.

Wound & Wound Toy Co.
7374 Melrose Avenue, Los Angeles
(323) 653-6703

L.A. Sociology 101

An often taken-for-granted L.A. phenomenon is our year-round yard sales. Yes, you heard it here—while most of the rest of the United States must wait impatiently for spring before they can hop in their car to drive insanely from house to house in search of treasure in the form of one man's junk, we L.A.-ites have the benefit of nearly constant warm weather, and thus, nearly a constant supply of yard sales. Some of the best areas to look are in the neighborhoods south of Melrose, in between Fairfax and La Brea, as well as all over the residential areas of Los Feliz and Silver Lake. Of course, as every geographical location has its norms, so does L.A. So you're not necessarily going to find your average Midwest fare of used Tupperware and blended fabric shirts at our yard bazaars. . . . No, the Los Angeles ones have been known to stock surfboards, giant Chinese lanterns, slot-machine paraphernalia, and plenty of used self-help tomes, which at one time guided all the onetime actors out of their rough patches; that is, before they decided to give it up for more secure digs as studio execs or caterers. So you, too, just might find a few Method-acting books and scripts (*lots* of old scripts) nestled in boxes or, if your proprietor was on the other end, a Super-8 camera or two.

Yard Sales
Year-round, all over

CHAPTER 11

Sundry Los Angeles

Miscellaneous Places Worth Checking Out

Now that's Infotainment! Billed as "the only state-wide television show in California about California," this wonderfully interesting half-hour-long show, hosted by a big teddy of a bear, Huell Howser, is chock-full of useful tourist information (and, in fact, outside of the realm of strip clubs and various other dens of iniquity, which *Gold* tends not to cover, the program usually does it better than most everyone except us). Most who know about *California's Gold* (even us Hollywood gossipcentric L.A.-ites) delight in watching the ever-optimistic buff, and undauntedly goofy Howser in his travels up and down the Western state in search of its history, its landmarks, its people, its fun, its surprising facts. We didn't know, for example, that the *Delta Queen*, which for over four decades was billed as one choice way to travel the Mississippi, was actually built here, in Stockton, California. Or that San Luis Obispo has a Chinatown. Or, coming a little closer to home, that See's Candies has a factory right here in L.A. *Mmm-mm.* Now we do. And we're certainly the wiser for it. In Los Angeles, the show airs on the weekdays at 7:30 P.M. on KCET Channel 13. But if you want to get in a few episodes before you get here, try the Web site, where you can order past shows for all your educational traveling needs (www.calgold.com).

California's Gold
Airs on KCET Channel 13, Monday–Friday at 7:30 P.M.; Sunday 7–8 P.M.

Sloppy Borders and the Trends of Evolution

How often I have been complimented on my photographs! How very often indeed. Most people would die to get half the compliments I receive. Yet I feel like the dead half of a Siamese twin. Why? Because it's not the orange-and-maroon crepuscule I shot in Budapest last spring that people laud, nor the only known photographs of that pygmy in Florence that nearly cost me a leg. No! It is the "sloppy borders" that amaze people. "My god, that is so striking, Chuck," they say. "Where do you get these photographs developed?" Once and for all, I will put it out there. Express Photo! Okay? Is that what you want? Are you satisfied? A little shop in a dinky mini-mall complex next to a 7-Eleven. They will apply those sloppy, fiesta-looking borders that make people feel spookily happy when they flip through the old album. As a tourist, you have the advantage of taking your Los Angeles–trip photos to Express Photo right across the street from Crossroads of America on Sunset and getting beautiful borders on your apparently irrelevant pictures. They can do it in an hour, if you want, but they will insist on sharing the spotlight with you. Like the time I took my famed shot of legendary novelist Stan Bolinowitz wearing the tiara, only to receive lukewarm responses. "Great border, though," said a tabloid I was trying to sell it to.

Catch the drift? On the plus side, the borders do enhance a mediocre shot, making it into something slightly spectacular. So there.

Express Photo
6660 Sunset Boulevard, Los Angeles
(323) 466-8437

Llamas with Underbites and Swans with Appetites

You know what, there is nothing like a good petting zoo when you're single, lacking values, or starving for attention. The Farm, in Reseda, aspires to more than your typical run-of-the-mill, eleven-animal petting zoos—*way* more. There are over one hundred barn friends to pet, paw, and feed, all of which have better manners than your average Angeleno. You can even take a pony ride, if you are so inclined—but there are no donkey shows just yet (don't ask, they don't think it's as funny as I do). The llamas have soft pelts and generally don't bite, and there are new piglets born all the time. Swans and ostriches eat directly from your cup ($2 for a large container; $1 for a smaller cup), while goats and sheep use their lips like vacuums sweeping your palms. Wolverines are all over the large farmyard, awaiting a petting, while chickens, ducks, pesky small children, and rabbits are constantly at your feet. Hell, when *Resident Tourist* visited, there were even cute little kittens curled up in a ball. They were all cuddly and shit. Not to mention a goat with rectangular pupils, which made us think, "Whoa, man, 'Shout at the devil!'" This is a perfect place to bring a date, the family, a mistress, or your cousin. Heavy petting costs more. (Just joshing about the wolverines.)

The Farm
8101 Tampa Avenue, Reseda
(818) 341-6805

Who Knew Rover Was in Pain?

Has this ever happened to you?

"Dear Lord, it has been thirty-nine hard-fought hours since Kitty last ate. What on earth should I do? Call a vet? . . . Force-feed her! She usually goes crackers over chilled Fancy Feast whitefish puree! Instead she hides her head in a stinky boot! Help me, god, help . . . ahhhh!" Sure it has. It has happened to all of us. Forget about the vet, they will put Kitty to sleep if you come at them with these kinds of problems. That's a certifiable fact. What you need is a nonverbal interspecies holistic healer who can get into Kitty's head, and see what's tampering with the poor feline's appetite. Enter Deborah Jones, an animal psychic and acupuncturist who, by use of mental imagery, communicates with your pet and/or animal friends. "I can put into words what the animal is feeling," says Deb. That's hard to dispute when the statistics are so positive in her favor (80 percent success rate). Animals communicate among themselves through mental images, and Deb knows how to penetrate the pelt and locate the source of an anxiety (such as new or unfamiliar surroundings after a move, new people in the house, a divorce, a death, other pets, etc.) or an injury. Animals are very instinctual and sensitive; therefore they must be recognized as such. So Deborah is a kind of a modern-day shaman who uses the mental images, or visualizations, cast by the subject pet to pinpoint the problem. Deb says her ability can be likened to communicating with infants or stroke victims, as a kind of universal language, if one merely learns it. No more, "Kitty is going to the vet [*sobbing violently*] . . . to be put to sleep [*sniff*]." Now you can chat with Kitty through an interpreter and see that Kitty just has a bad case of gas from eating table scraps. Deborah is available for half-hour ($75) and full-hour ($125) consultations, and can conduct sessions over the phone. Or visit www.animalshealing.com, to learn more about Deb and what she does. Monday–Friday office hours.

Deborah Jones (Nonverbal Interspecies Communicator)
228½ Howland Canal, Venice
(310) 305-1552

Ye of Little Faith

You down with God? *Resident Tourist* will now dip its curious toes into the tepid waters of religion and offer you this curve. Narrow-mindedness is hardly becoming, mind you, especially where so much Universe is concerned—so the good people at The Neighborhood Church in Pasadena have the broadness to embrace all active religions in one place of worship. The Neighborhood Church believes in a "Unitarian Universalist," which is the backer of a common God for all, or a common spirit, or a common love (without the peyote [optional], and with no occultism). It is a support system with an open policy. But it is a community foremost, with a church, a separate chapel, a parish school, and classrooms for children, a community center, a kiosk board of support groups, and classes (yoga, political, etc.), and a woodsy feel under the green pines of southern California. Founded in 1887, this is the oldest standing church in Pasadena. It hails itself as a "Liberal Religious Community" that stands for love instead of prejudice in all capacities. The open-belief policy is actually a way of better understanding theology in general, and finding yourself in the process. In no way are there any pressures or ultimatums to live up to, just the therapeutic inner peace that paying homage to the Creator can bring. *Resident Tourist* does not want to act as evangelist, or as persuader, but it does want to point out alternatives to standard beliefs so we can sleep soundly at night. Because hey, we care. And check this out, the hot wood aroma of the church floorboards smells like a warm sauna with those soothing heat rocks. See? It is like a mini-resort (www. uuneighborhood.com).

The Neighborhood Church
301 N. Orange Grove Boulevard, Pasadena
(626) 449-3470

But It's Only Make-Believe, Little Grill

It may look like any other house in this lovely West Hollywood neighborhood. In reality, it's party central for children. Olivia's

Doll House Tea Room houses the party stuff of little girls' dreams, with frills for days. Dress up till you can't see straight, using all their costumes: dresses, wraps, character outfits, shoes, hats, boas, purses . . . Each party has its own attendant to do nails, hair, and makeup, adding to the glamour. A three-course lunch is served, and, of course, birthday cake. The birthday girl gets to choose from the birthday toy chest, and each child gets a photo in all her finery. The Tea Room must be booked months in advance, as there is a limited number of parties per day. There's a minimum of six children, but up to twenty-seven can be accommodated. It's a dream day for the lucky birthday girl, and the quality is top-notch. The cost for all this is $250 for six deliriously happy party-goers. There is an additional charge of $25 per child for more than six children.

Olivia's Doll House Tea Room
8804 Rosewood, West Hollywood
(310) 273-6631

Feelin' Cool, Paying Little

The Sunset Strip is a relentless, money-sucking vortex that takes, takes, takes, and often gives back nothing much in return—unless you count a long wait in traffic on Friday nights or a hang-over on Saturday. Most credit-conscious residents not driving BMWs or wearing shiny black shirts try to avoid setting foot on it if at all possible. But then, the Strip, for all its sins, is still pretty cool. Where else can you look through a giant piece of glass down into the rest of the city while lounging on an enormous bed near a pool and sipping an Irish coffee (Sky Bar)? Or catch sight of—we're sure James Dean would have been better—Keanu Reeves seated at a bar, imbibing coffee all by his lonesome (Bar Marmont)? But then, of course, if you show up at these places, you're expected, again, to drop a lot of dough. There is one place on the Strip, however, that you can come out of feeling pretty darn cool without having given up too much: Rudy's Barbershop. Located inside the Standard Hotel (a larger Rudy's, inside what looks like an old garage, can be found a little west of here), this vintage kitsch salon originated in Seattle and comes complete with magazine rack and plenty of 1960s-style adornments. Rudy's charges only about $20—not bad for L.A.; great for Sunset—for a standard haircut (women's styles, of course, are a little more). Walking out onto the Strip after having one of Rudy's well-trained lads or lasses do up your hair, you're sure to feel as cool as any old L.A. cat.

Rudy's Barbershop
8300 Sunset Boulevard, West Hollywood
(323) 650-5669
Also:
4451 W. Sunset Boulevard, Los Angeles
(323) 661-6535

Giving and Receiving

For my dollar, there is no better place to beg or give change than at the 7-Eleven at Yucca and Cahuenga. A healthy rotation of homeless (and nonhomeless) people frequent the corner there, some with ratty curs and/or children. If you like philanthropy, go drop a nickel into the hands of an actual "English" urchin (who lives in an apartment on Yucca, I've seen her!) or a small band of broke, thirsty men with beer guts. You'll feel less guilty about that ice-cream sandwich you bought if you do. There is one man who talks in tongues; another shouts real loud and, if I am not mistaken, said something about an apocalyptic womb! The panhandlers there are actually quite honest, too. Some want food, some want alcohol, some want drugs, some want diapers for their children. It is random that way. And fun! One night I even gave some Dots candies to a group of punk-rock kids who were like, "Right on, man—anarchy!" You bet! For those of you who are looking to make some good coin panhandling, I would advise you to get there early, as the corner fills up quickly. An Israeli man who asked to remain anonymous said, "You can make a good fifty bucks in a couple of hours," and I am not gullible. You see—honesty!

7-Eleven
1910 N. Cahuenga Boulevard at Yucca
Open 24 hours

The Real Wax Museum

At first it seemed unusual that a zany, fun-colored children's salon would harbor a waxing studio in the rear, but then again, it makes perfect sense. Check it: Mom goes and gets waxed while young Billy gets that Matchbox 20 cut that is sure to catch the attention of that blond sass in third-hour Social Studies. That is the concept over at The Yellow Balloon children's salon and Andrea's Waxing Studio. The former is a red-and-yellow carnival with the smell of popcorn in the air and takes anyone from toddlers to adolescent teens getting their crops cut into a precious or ultracool style. The stylists are a perfect daycare bunch, who occasionally read the likes of Bulgakov, and they know how to entertain a child. Meanwhile the latter venue, Andrea's, takes down unwanted leg and armpit hair, mustaches, and overgrown subregions where the sun don't shine. To put it more bluntly, she solves hygiene problems, okay, Chewbacca? Andrea's terminology is innovative and uncommonly accurate, and revered by celebrities and maternal/paternal types alike. Choose from "the Brazilian," or the "chin rest," as Andrea calls it (a small triangular tuft), "the playboy" (a thin Mohawk), or the "Full Monty" wax (bald is beautiful) when reconfiguring your southerly treasures. It is relatively painless, because Andrea is a pro. And so are those hairdressers out front, who do everything shy of juggling to make haircuts eventful for kids. Oedipus couldn't have dreamed up a more ideal setting himself.

The Yellow Balloon
12130 Ventura Boulevard, Studio City
(818) 760–7141
Andrea's Waxing Studio
12130 Ventura Boulevard, Studio City
(818) 985–WAXX [9299]

CHAPTER 12

Entertainment in Los Angeles

Animal Crackers Make . . . Evil?

The ACME Comedy Theater is a multiplex of wonder, where clownery is given a red carpet and writers seriously *hope* people laugh in their face when they come up with an idea. Plus there is valet parking. The name of the game here is comedy—sketch comedy, like *Saturday Night Live* . . . only it's funny. Splitting guts and reddening knees is what this theatrical troupe lives for. Forget about Groundlings, the Laugh Factory, and the Comedy Store, though they all have had their moments; this is a new wave of comedy: harder-edged, more erudite, less hammy (no water-squirting carnations or "blonde" jokes here). It is where comedic genius germinates, comes together, and eventually takes over television. The list of past and present ACME members is impressive, ranging from *Loveline*'s Adam Carolla, Fred Willard, Wil Wheaton,

Brad Sherwood, and Ryan Stiles, to up-and-comers Billy Wright (brilliant as Chore Boy) and Robert Yasumura. The list goes on relentlessly, forever and ever. All of them have acted and/or written for sketch-comedy shows, studying under the tutelage of the wizard, M. D. Sweeney. Essentially, this is a training camp for serious writers and comedians to hone their craft in front of live audiences. ACME was a synagogue once upon a time, which makes one ponder theology and laugh simultaneously, the way God drew it up on his parchment some two *hundred* years ago. It is now a 99-seat theater, where audience members convulse with idiotic laughter without repercussions, never having to bite their lips. The intermission tag-team drummer and keyboard players have something special going on between them, too, something eerily puritanical. They are lithe and stellar, like the average red fox. It is a well-oiled machine, ACME is, with daring comedy and plenty of inspiration. You'll feel like watching George Burns in *Oh God!* again.

ACME Comedy Theater
135 N. La Brea Avenue, Los Angeles
(323) 993-5778, or (323) 525-0233 for information
regarding the Comedy School

Fights Away from the Cacophonous Hoi Polloi

You can always go to Dublin's and push your way through the cramped line (and once inside, push your way into the cramped beer bar line) to watch a title bout on one of their many TVs, along with the rest of the loud, Sunset Strip post-college jock-and-betty types. Or, for that matter, you can cram yourself into any other of the various meat-market bars L.A. has to offer to see the big fight, if you're into that sort of thing. Of course, one classy alternative for your Tyson rumble is The Barbershop Club on Melrose. This exquisite, 1940s-style haircutters' salon (by appointment only), used to feature weekly parties until owner Woody saw they were getting way too big and out-of-hand. These days, the Club has the occasional nighttime get-together, which includes many of the big sports events. And since the policy is BYOB, there's no lame lines to contend with.

The Barbershop Club
6907 Melrose Avenue, Los Angeles
(323) 939-4319
For more information and schedule, go to www.
barbershopclub.com

Blessing of the Animals, Including the Jackalope

This is a spectacular and heartwarming sight. Each year since 1930, on Holy Saturday, the day before Easter, animal-lovers descend upon Olvera Street, pets and livestock in tow, for the magical Blessing of the Animals. Children come with their turtles in little plastic boxes and fish in their bowls, along with birds, dogs, chickens, donkeys, kittens, pigs, and . . . oh, yes, one huge albino python. Everyone's dressed for the occasion, including the animals, colorful with flowers and ribbons. As the procession rounds the plaza, Cardinal Roger Mahoney, sprinkling holy water, bestows the blessings upon the animals. All the newly blessed animals continue the procession, which snakes through the plaza. It's quite the celebration and an expression of just how much people care for their animal companions. It's a marvelous tradition and attracts quite a crowd, many of whom do not bring their pets, but come to be a part of this special observance. It's a timeless recognition of how much animals have given to the human race.

Blessing of the Animals
Olvera Street, Downtown
(213) 625-5045
Saturday before Easter Sunday

The Camera Adds Weight, My Eye

"That little thing?" I asked my sister, who had put the car in park. "Yep, that's it," she answered. I had to believe her, for yes, there was that inimitable triangular slope of a roof, the brown shingles, the ranch-style offshoot to the right of the triangle. But it looked much smaller than I remembered it. And there was something else. . . . We were idling in my sister's BMW (L.A. has been good to her, though with all the BMWs in this city, one has to wonder if L.A. is not good to everyone) on Dilling Street in the Valley, directly across from the house at address 11222, the one where the Brady Bunch "lived." Somehow it was different, though. What was it? "The fence wasn't there on the show," my sister said, as if reading my mind. (I later read that the current owner—no, not Mike Brady—of twenty years put the guardrail around to keep all the curiosity-seekers at bay.) After a long pause, I relented: "Okay, yes, that's the house." "That's what I said," she answered, and we both began humming the tune from the show.

The Brady Bunch House, 11222 Dilling Street, North Hollywood

Death Can Be Fun

Before it became the marketing machine it is, Halloween had roots in an ancient Celtic custom which saw townsfolk donning ghoulish costumes to ward off evil spirits come to possess the living. Over the years, the Mexican holiday Día de los Muertos (Day of the Dead) has evolved, too. Originated more than three thousand years ago by Meso-American Indians such as the Aztecs and the Mayans, Día de los Muertos was originally observed at the end of summer. The ceremonies lasted up to twenty days and included memorials for the souls of passed adults and children both. During the years before the conquests, however, the dates were changed by arrogant Spanish missionaries so that they coincided with the Christian holidays All Saints' Day and All Souls' Day, which fall on November 1 and 2, respectively. The souls of dead children, or *angelitos*, were then honored on November 1, while adults were remembered the following day. Christian symbols were later added to the intricate altars, known as *ofrendas*, erected to remember the deceased. L.A., a city steeped in Mexican culture (must have *something* to do with the great Mexican population here), has many Day of the Dead celebrations to offer, but the best one tends to be on Olvera Street, the ostensible birthplace of the city. The merchants there host daylong celebrations at the beginning of November, where revelers walk around in skeletal faces imbibing alcohol and washing it down with the free bread, known as *Pan de Muerto*. And since these days are supposed to honor the dead with celebration, they usually focus a lot less on the somber stuff and keep it simply a good old time; it's a little like Halloween in that manner.

Day of the Dead Celebration
November 1 and 2, at Olvera Street, Downtown

Vintage Theaters for Family Fun
This most exquisite theater, refurbished to perfection and at great expense by Disney and Theaters, is a wonder. El Capitán is the exclusive first-run theater for Disney releases; it's well worth a viewing. And they serve Hebrew National hot dogs, because only the best will do here. There's an organist who plays the mighty Wurlitzer, regaling the waiting crowd with Disney showtunes. When the lights go down, so does he, disappearing beneath the stage. For extra-special premieres, they'll take over the building next door and create a fantastic playland, with three floors of things to do. For *102 Dalmatians*, one entire room was a moon bouncer *and* they had Krispy Kreme doughnuts. In the past they've featured a *Disney's Saturday Mornings at the Movies* program, with sing-alongs, contests, and live music. The El Capitán has also done some midnight-movie sing-alongs for adults, à la *Rocky Horror*. *Mary Poppins* has been featured, as has *Evita*, to great success. Fans come dressed as their favorite character, they throw things at the screen, and sing along with gusto. Keep an eye out for the next one. El Capitán is directly across Hollywood Boule-

vard from the brand-new Hollywood and Highland Complex featuring the Kodak Theater, new home of the Oscars. It's also right across from the famed Graumann's Chinese Theater, with all the foot- and handprints, which has also gotten quite a facelift as part of the huge redevelopment of the area. The El Capitán was one of a trio of themed theaters developed by original Hollywood moguls Charles Toberman and Sid Graumann. The Chinese, which bore Graumann's name, and the El Capitán were joined by the Egyptian, which has also undergone detailed restoration recently and is in pristine condition. The Egyptian is the home of American Cinémathèque, and is the scene of many fascinating festivals, speakers, and classic films. At the Chinese, you'll not only see the famed footprints, but there are usually any number of celebrity impersonator/street performers ready for their close-ups. Take a step back in time to a more opulent moviegoing experience with any one of these three landmarks.

El Capitán Theater
6834 Hollywood Boulevard, Hollywood
(323) 467-7674
www.elcapitantickets.com

Graumann's Chinese Theater
6925 Hollywood Boulevard, Hollywood
www.manntheaters.com

The Egyptian Theater
Hollywood Boulevard, Hollywood
(323) 461-2020
www.americancinematheque.com

Halloween Ain't for Wimps

WARNING: The annual Halloween Hollywood Costume Carnival on Santa Monica Boulevard in West Hollywood is not for the claustrophobic or the homophobic. And if you're thinking about just throwing on a pair of fangs and pale makeup and going as a vampire, you'll most certainly end up feeling underdressed or, at the least, hopelessly uncreative. One year, a tamer group of about ten people went as an actual museum, wearing frames around their heads and representing, to a tee, the *Mona Lisa*, the *American Gothic* pitchfork-carrying farmer and his daughter, and van Gogh's *Self-portrait*—complete with lopped–off–ear improvisation—from behind these frames. A modern-art mobile made of the remaining five or six of the group, picked up the rear. And with the usual contingency of bearded cross-dressers, queens, lesbians, S&M types, epicene aliens, and raging drunks, this mad bacchanalia might make those who are less secure with their sexuality pray their friends didn't see them on the nine o'clock news covering the event. But hot damn—for the rest of you, you're really in for the best row since Mardi Gras; but better, because, since it's in the very nice WeHo area, you don't get the same public urination problems as in New Orleans.

Annual Halloween Hollywood Costume Carnival, on October 31
Santa Monica Boulevard between Doheny Drive and La Cienaga Boulevard, West Hollywood

During the Day, a Fun-Packed Bowl

Sure, with its stacked parking and big crowd–drawing acts, a nighttime visit to The Hollywood Bowl to see the reunited Jane's Addiction, for example, can be a somewhat painful experience. But then, of course, most big-name concert events in any town include healthy smatterings of joy and frustration. Our advice on this? Whether it's Barbra Streisand at the Staples Center or Lynyrd Skynyrd at Pine Knob in Michigan, when packing your bong and a warm coat for the event, you'd do best also to bring along your ability to count to ten. As for the Bowl, may we suggest something a little different? Arrive early and leave before the concert starts. What's that? you say. Well, let us explain. The Hollywood Bowl, which sits in a dugout with naturally excellent acoustics and holds both the L.A. Philharmonic and its own classical pops orchestra, is also a lush park with plenty of grass, thus making it the perfect place to picnic; or to just plain hang out (the Bowl also offers a good array of foods at its restaurant or concession stands). If you come early enough—a little after nine A.M. is about right—during the summer months (the Bowl is closed from October to May anyhow), you may even get to catch a glimpse of the orchestra rehearsals that go on there. Barring this, a quiet afternoon with your lover or even occasionally irksome family members on a hill, is much better, you must admit, than a loud evening steeped with logistical annoyances. But if you must see Journey or Aerosmith, we aren't going to stop you, either.

The Hollywood Bowl
2301 N. Highland Avenue, Los Angeles
(323) 851-3588

A Parade Rings Home Christmas!

This parade is held annually, the Sunday after Thanksgiving. Yes, it's kooky and kitschy, loaded with celebrities from the A, B, and C lists. You've got your floats, your bands, and it's the official kickoff for the holidays in Hollywood. The street decorations are up, the air feels festive—what the heck? You can buy grandstand seats, or just find some space along the parade route and set up camp. The parade begins in front of Graumann's Chinese Theater, of course, and goes east to Vine. It then heads south to Sunset Boulevard and west to La Brea Avenue. Streets in the area are closed well in advance, so if you're planning anything in Hollywood that day, do it on foot and park well away, otherwise you're trapped or your car gets towed. It's a fun night, usually chilly, in a southern California sort of way. The streets are bedecked with holiday lights and tinsel, ensuring a festive time for all.

Hollywood Christmas Parade
(323) 469-2337
Sunday after Thanksgiving
www.hollywoodchristmas.com

Brass Lungs

If you're looking for a place to watch and better appreciate live jazz, The Jazz Bakery will serve you brilliantly. Many a legend has passed through the former Helms Bakery, for no other reason than to do what they love: playing music. The Jazz Bakery is a nonprofit organization, whose sole mission is to stage jazz music seven nights a week, in a school-like auditorium. The scene is intimate, and the acts are never disappointing. Artists like Terence Blanchard, Elvin Jones, T. S. Monk (Thelonious' son), and the late Joe Henderson have come through with their bands and left their mark. You will see why the Beat poets went apeshit back in the 1950s over Charlie Parker and the whole jazz scene. These cats have something to say, and they do it with bloodshot eyes and hoarse voices. And they say it through saxophones, trumpets, pianos, and stand-up basses. Alfy is a small gold dog that serves as the joint's mascot. He is the very picture of cool, usually sitting in the ticket window. Pet him at your leisure; he don't bite (hard). There's also a coffee bar and cold beer to purchase, along with montage artwork on the walls to view during breaks. Everything is wide open and full of promise here, a general retro feeling in the spirit. And then the madmen play. And the madmen cast their spell.

The Jazz Bakery
1836 Benedict Canyon Drive, Beverly Hills
(310) 271-9039

Gay Pride Celebration and Parade

Held in the latter portion of June, this is actually the "Christopher Street West" Lesbian, Gay, Bi-Sexual and Transgender Pride Celebration—known as LGBT Pride. It's a huge festival and parade, where West Hollywood is descended upon by hundreds of thousands of people. It's colorful, it's musical, it's loads of fun and full of festivities. The festival runs Saturday and Sunday, and the parade is Sunday morning. For the festival, San Vincente Boulevard is closed off to traffic and lined with hundreds of booths from a variety of businesses and organizations. Lots of tents with DJs playing all sorts of music, dancing, entertainment . . . for hours upon hours. The parade on Sunday is routed down Santa Monica Boulevard and is a frenzy, with an absolutely enormous crowd. The sun, the scene—it's a great taste of pure West Hollywood pride.

LGBT Pride
West Hollywood at San Vincente and Santa Monica
Boulevards
Lapride.org

Fiery Bingo for the Eccentric Within You

Once a weekly happening, Legendary Bingo is now played monthly. Event-guy extraordinaire Jeffrey Bowman's Legendary Bingo has raised, as of this writing, over $150,000 for local charities. And if you think bingo is sedate and serious, this will knock you sideways. The charming and razor-sharp "Belle Aire" is your bingo hostess, and yes, she's a drag queen. If you make her mad by not paying attention, or talking when she is, she'll make you come up front for a paddling, bingo-style. She's joined each week by a celebrity ball-caller, all of whom do a great job of keeping up with her. Tina Yothers, Patrika Darbo, Jim J. Bullock, and Jeff Probst have all spun balls with Belle. It started out as Drag Queen Bingo at a small coffeehouse in West Hollywood and has traveled around town for special appearances at major events, but remains a neighborhood force in raising both funds for charity and the eyebrows of "bingo virgins," as Belle Aire calls first-timers. You can win terrific prizes, but the real prize is that you're playing for a good cause, every time. It's raunchy, it's loud, it's wildly fun. Check out www.legendarybingo.com for the Celebrity Ball Caller Hall of Fame; the Many and Various Hair Moods of the Fabulous Belle Aire; and links to all the charities that have benefited from the generosity of rabid bingo players and fans.

Legendary Bingo

8571 Santa Monica Boulevard, West Hollywood

(310) 659-7009

Monthly, call for date

www.legendarybingo.com (to confirm location)

You Should Be So Lucky (or Magical)

Unlike the many exclusive clubs in Los Angeles that seem to base admittance on youth and good looks, The Magic Castle is ostensibly an old boys' club. And the place literally reeks of money, face-lifts, polyester, and dust (and a goodly amount of Victorian mystique of the often-gaudy variety). Still, if you should be so lucky as to have a member (probably an Academy of Magical Arts, Inc., member and thus a magician who had to pass a special test) as a friend, by all means don't pass up his (or her—yes, there are some female members) invitation to dine at the Castle. Alternatively, if someone hands you a special "get-in" card, do follow the rules on the back and go. Be warned: You are in for an overpriced meal (unless you decide not to magically appear for your reservation . . . *hint, hint*). However, the magic acts—of the close-up, prestidigitation, and grandiose, cape-wearing David Copperfield variety—are excellent. In addition, a "ghostly" piano player in the downstairs bar takes requests—we suggested "Imagine" by John Lennon, and sure enough, the invisible "Irma" played it (though later we wished we had asked for something a little less piano-friendly, such as Warrant's "Cherry Pie"). And the 25-cent ambient sound machine located in the bathroom next to the phone ("Honey, I'll be a little late. I'm at the office/stuck in traffic/etc.") is good fun. So is the dungeon tour, which includes glimpses of plastic skeletons covered in fake cobwebs. Fun stuff.

The Magic Castle

7001 Franklin Avenue, Los Angeles

(323) 851-3313

www.magiccastle.com

Revival Reminds Me of Church

Don't know about you folks, but I always wanted to see *The Shining* on the big screen, but I was still pooping green when it came out. Oh sure, there was a time when I was five years old that the parents would play the tape for me while they went out swinging at night at one key party or another—but that is not the same as watching Jack Nicholson on the big screen plotting the amiably brutal deaths of his immediate family. Sound familiar? Worry not, reader: There are now "revival houses" to allow you the chance of seeing that movie you missed back then. New Beverly Cinema is a favorite of *Resident Tourist*, because, frankly, it is close by. The theater itself takes suggestions for movies you would like to see played there, and puts out a two-month calendar of upcoming films they intend to show. The movies are always double or triple features of past great movies and/or obscurities with common links to one another (i.e., director, theme, foreign, lead actor . . . something). It is a measly $6 admission, and the theater is as uncomfortable as any other theater that charges $9 and upward for movies that are untested and predominantly unsatisfying. We like Woody Allen and Monty Python, and New Beverly plays these. We also like porn, but no luck there.

New Beverly Cinema
7165 Beverly Boulevard, Los Angeles
(323) 938-4038

All That Celebrity Has Me Seeing Stars

Hollywood is a land of glamour and magic, as you probably already know—you poor deprived souls with movie-watcher cards and silver-screen idols! That's why you either visit Los Angeles, or you live out here. Why else would you photograph a filthy sidewalk with Bob Hope's name inside a star? What could be more gratifying than seeing the big stars (like actor/game show host Ben Stein and Mickey Rourke) in the process of making the same Hollywood films that had Wichita and Des Moines all soiling their britches? Well, the Web has a handy site where you can go and find any L.A.-based movies being filmed on location. Hollywood magic has never been dealt such a blow. Who knew that the Cobra Kai Dojo from the original *Karate Kid* was in North Hollywood, *not* Reseda, as the film would have you believe? See? Hollywood magic! The Web site is www.seeing-stars.com. Punch in a particular movie, and the site searches out the location for you. Say hello to "the Brawny Man" and Julia Stiles, who *Resident Tourist* would love to see in a movie together real soon.

www.seeing-stars.com

Now That's Entertainment

Drama, murder, mystery, and a happy ending are all included in The Silent Movie Theater's tale. Originally opened in 1942 by John and Dorothy Hampton, the theater abruptly closed in the late 1970s—some say due to the lung cancer Mr. Hampton contracted from the chemicals he used to restore the old film footage before it went on the screen. The theater was reopened in 1991 after a family friend, Lawrence Austin, convinced Mrs. Hampton, ailing with Alzheimer's, to let him take over the venue's management. However, in 1997 Austin's lover, apparently seeing an inheritance opportunity, hired a young thug to kill Austin. In January of 1997, Christian Rodriguez, at the behest of James Van Sickle, took in a show and afterward, fatally shot Austin. The two co-conspirators were subsequently sentenced to life, and the theater closed once again. Serendipitously, Santa Monica songwriter Charlie Lustman was in the neighborhood for a bite to eat a few years back when he stumbled on the chained-up, for-sale theater. Undaunted by the theater's tragic past, he bought it, had an expert clear it of its ghosts in a bizarre smudging ritual, and refurbished it beautifully, opening it up to audiences again in 1999. Lustman added an upstairs café, in addition to the standard concession stand, behind which young employees in vintage garb smile as they sell you popcorn and Coke at modern-day prices. Yes, some things have changed over the years—even here. Still, for the $9 adult admission price, people are treated to much more than what they get at your modern-day, "load 'em in, clear 'em out" movie houses. On some nights, Lustman himself takes the stage before a showing and belts out a song about the virtues of the silent era, and at intermission, prizes are thrown to the smarter members of the audience who can answer silent-movie trivia questions. And though the old movies are generally shorter, the audience is treated to a round of shorts before the headliner; there's *Felix the Cat* and *The Little Rascals* before they were talkies, just to name a few. All of this is set to live organ music, played by the in-house musician, making for an experience convincing us that, yes, they don't make 'em like they used to. Also, in an interesting twist, there are plans for a movie on the history of the theater, including the murder.

The Silent Movie Theater
611 N. Fairfax Avenue, Los Angeles
(323) 655-2520

A Grand Evening

While standing in line at the post office a few years back, actor-writer DeLauné Michel realized there was a certain void in L.A.; and so she decided to fill it. In May of 1996 she hosted her first "Spoken Interludes," a deliciously bourgeois dinner party featuring post-meal readings of poetry and story excerpts from a variety of local authors and actors. Since then and at various venues (it does look like Tempest on Santa Monica might be a permanent resting place), she has toastmistressed her fun monthly soirées for martini-sipping adults (usually the third Sunday of every month). At the last event, which featured a couple of tasty pasta dishes set up buffet-style, Winona Ryder wasn't able to show up; nonetheless, the larger-than-life Camryn Manheim did an absolutely funny and heartrending (at one point, tears sprung forth from her eyes) reading of Jennifer Weiner's *Good in Bed*, about an overweight girl who, in the scene read, faces an ex-boyfriend who published an article about dating her fat self. As well, the charmingly English Brian Cox of *L.I.E.* and *Rushmore* (just to name a few) did Charles Siebert's *Angus*, while director Roland Joffe (*The Mission, The Killing Fields*), for his part, read from his own work, *The Importance of Kissing*; other guests were local magazine magnate Joie Davidow, who read from her *Marked for Life*; and Mark Salzman, whose wonderful setup comparing the faith-based natures of religion and artistry ended with a reading of his *Lying Awake*, about a contemplative nun who finds religious inspiration at the cost of a strange brain disease named after Dostoyevsky, which is characterized by intense feelings of a higher purpose.

Spoken Interludes
Once a month at Tempest Supper Club
7323 Santa Monica Boulevard, Los Angeles
(323) 957-4688
For more information, go to www.spokeninterludes.com

Rockin' and Definitely Rollin'

The phrase "this is the most fun you can have with your clothes on" is custom-made for World on Wheels' monthly adult (of the hippest kind) roller-skating party; that is, of course, if you can keep from falling flat on your ass, which many people, rusty since the '70s, do. But then, the sweet buzz you can get at Wheels' upstairs bar—adjacent to the bowling alley—will certainly help to pad any pains you receive at least until the next morning. So, you're basically in the clear to have a raucous and retro good time, despite your gawky, uncoordinated self.

The DJs here spin the kind of tunes that will make you long for the days when hyper stitched Jordaches and the obligatory comb in the back pocket (used to create a perfect feathered do) were the required uniform. And the rink's centrally located wall-to-wall-rugged lounging area is smooth as hell, even if you can't bring your drinks there (this ain't fricking *Looking for Mr. Goodbar* meets *Rollerderby*—please!) The party starts every fourth Saturday at ten P.M. and lasts until two A.M.; the $10 admission fee includes skate rental. But if you're bad enough, you'll already have your own pair strung across your shoulders on the way in. For more information, go to www.rollerdisco. goodfoot.org.

World on Wheels
4645½ Venice Boulevard, Los Angeles
(323) 933-3333

Free Concert: Bring Your Own Percussion Instruments

Ah, Venice Beach. This little strip of oceanfront land between Santa Monica and Marina Del Rey is a strange, time-warped place where hippie throwbacks mesh with prepubescent punker delinquents, agape-eyed tourists, health-conscious Rollerbladers, and bad-ass gang members. It's an oasis for worldwise wanderers, charlatan street performers, longhaired protesters, drunken hummers of Jimmy Buffett songs, and the schizoid homeless. It's like a slightly more malevolent (must we remind one, here is where the Doors came from?) Grateful Dead concert with no Jerry Garcia (but a lot of look-alikes). And what's a Dead concert without a drum circle? Well, it's a sandwich without the bread, a sundae without the cherry on top. Never you worry—for here, you get your bread and cherries, too. For years, the Venice Beach Drum Circle—made up of many of the above types and more—has, every Saturday and Sunday from midafternoon until after Sunset, given the strange brew of humanity who visit and dwell here their free tunage. It's an often-spiritual experience in which a hodgepodge of real and makeshift percussionists gather on the beach to make their heavily layered beats, while dervishlike dancers skirt the perimeter, twirling and raising their hands to the heavens. It's really something to see, hear, taste, and touch (should you be bold enough to get involved; "the more, the merrier" is the circle's motto). In recent years the drumming has occasionally come under attack from peeved residents, creating a dialogue at city hall and rendering the future of the circle uncertain. So check it out while you still can.

Venice Beach Drum Circle
Venice Beach
For information go to www.venicebeachdrumcircle.com

Long Beach's Habitat for Huge Manatees

Okay, there are no manatees at the Long Beach Aquarium of the Pacific (this isn't Florida!), but there are plenty of sea lions, yellowfin tuna, puffins, barracuda, sea otters, and aqua-orbital jellies. Basically, this aquarium is dedicated to everything in the Pacific. If you have ever taken a long look at a sea dragon, a kind of gossamer seahorse that is more like a diminutive fire-breather with leafy appendages, then you have looked into the infinite beauty of life itself. Try calling them by their scientific name, *Phycodurus equus,* and impress your friends. Peer into the homestead of the giant Japanese spider crabs in their natural environment and feel a little bit like a Peeping Tom. Look hard enough at the sea otters during their mating season and feel downright voyeuristic. All of the exhibits and habitats have placards to help explain, define, and describe what it is you are looking at. How else to know the life span of the sea turtle or to determine how the diving birds of the Bering Sea avoid catching cough due to cold in the frigid waters? The sea lion exhibit is a great place to rest your dogs and have refreshments while a chipper guide explains the differences between seals and sea lions. Concentrate on the anchovy tank. Wow, these poor bastards are confined to swimming eternal laps in that tubular glass tank, yawning uncontrollably the whole time. Better than being a pizza topping or a meal for the bottom-feeding sheepshead with a fishhook through your nose, I suppose.

Long Beach Aquarium of the Pacific
100 Aquarium Way, Long Beach
(562) 590-3100

Vine Theater, You've Got One Friend

Now that the Beverly Theater, which used to offer second-run blockbusters at a discount rate of $2.75, has been bought up by Laemmle and turned into an art house, we have nary a place to turn for cheap movie seats in the city anymore. It's no minuscule shame either, with admission costing upward of 8 bucks these days (to say nothing for the expensive tubs of synthetic butter–soaked Styrofoam we end up getting to go with our syrupy $4 Coca-Colas). But then, ladies and gentlemen, that's the general state of cinema entertainment in the big city. You want to see, you gotta, er, pay, in other words. Luckily, that's not all, folks. The Vine Theater on Hollywood Boulevard is not exactly as pretty as the Beverly Center (nor is it exactly as ugly in the same way as the Center's tubey parking structure), but it does have cheap seats. Nestled near a couple of sex shops, a tattoo parlor, and a vinyl-record store, it offers mostly second-run double features for the low, low price of (drum roll, please) just 5 measly buckaroonies. And sometimes it gets the first-run stuff within a week or two of release. If one is willing to slum a little, this is a perfect place to get out of the sun or, at night, away from all the boulevard panhandlers to catch a glimpse of your favorite celluloid star.

Vine Theater
6321 Hollywood Boulevard, Los Angeles
(323) 463-1819

CHAPTER 13

Don't Leave Yet—You Just Gotta See This Los Angeles

As the Stomach Turns—L.A. Traffic, Public Transportation, Useful Services, and More!

Road rage. Traffic jams. Sig Alerts (see next page). Passive drivers. Welcome, folks, to L.A., a city whose public transportation system moves as many people daily as live in Philadelphia but still looks like a snarled mess of automobiles from above, and often feels like a splitting headache from behind the wheel. The drivers here are so slow to react sometimes as to seem broken, rendered baying sheep by years of waiting in long auto queues with no immediate end in sight. This may also explain the general laid-back, it's-all-good mentality outsiders tend to throw on the population here—because of our traffic woes, we have learned quickly the lesson that many aspects of life are beyond our control. Or maybe we're so mellow because unlike, say, in New York, we don't have as much opportunity to hop on a train and read about all the problems in the world to our hearts' discontent.

Whatever the case, the freeways are the worst, possibly because they're expected by most to be the best, that is, to be actual fast venues for transporting one from one place to the next. Many the day we've sat for what seems like hours on the 405 or the 10 West, in what AM radio hosts here call Sig Alerts, those reports passed down from the California Highway Patrol noting crappy traffic conditions. These have made us want to ram our cars into the driver next us, if only to relieve the mad tension of the wait. Others fight the problem by simply popping a book on tape into their decks or by chatting on their cell phones, which may or may not make matters worse.

The less technically equipped and calmer of us often resort to simple escape, i.e., reverie—if only an imaginary road above the one I'm driving on would appear before me and I could take it directly home, or wouldn't it be cool if the city forefathers had foreseen all the trouble and built giant freeway-side parking lots where bands like Blink 182 or the Offspring played until traffic cleared?—you could just pop your California driver's license into the turnstile and get a free show to ease your tensed mind. But alas . . .

Though the general belief is that you simply must have a car if you live in L.A. (another, diametrically opposed one is that with the smog test fees and the expensive yearly registering process, one has to be a veritable millionaire to even own a car here), the Metropolitan Transportation Authority does have its usefulness. And, as residents who have now and then been without our driving machines, we can say that the system in L.A., if a little daunting and unwieldy, is quite satisfactory. Of course, we don't suggest you tourists plan on taking the general city buses if at all possible, as they don't, with their numerous lines, always make for the most concise trip (nor do they come without their strange array of smells). But there are a few particularly good forms of public transpo in this city that are worth noting, even for you, our dear tourist.

With all its one-way streets, Downtown driving can be a real hassle. So may we suggest the Dash service, which for a mere 25 cents (one free transfer) will tote you around to some of the more well-known spots in the city from Little Tokyo, to Chinatown, to L.A.'s corridors of power, to the Grand Central Market, to the Central Library. And, surprise, these Dash buses tend to be clean, air-conditioned, and, very often, not as crowded as the other city buses; and, bonus: since the Downtown area is somewhat small compared to other cities, these go about their business quite quickly. Our suggestion is that if you have to go Downtown, drive there (don't forget the first rule of getting there: use back-streets with abandon) and park at one spot. Then take these little gems—stops and schedules are numerous and quite visible—to all the places you need to go.

Another beneficial service is the city's underused and much-maligned Red Line subway system, which is by no means extensive but does have some of the more notable tourist stops on its route. Starting at the beautiful and historic (hint, hint: check it out) Union Station Downtown, it runs near the Wiltern Theatre, Hollywood and Vine (by the Pantages Theater, where *Lion King* has been all the rage these days), to the Hollywood and Highland Complex (very close to Mann's Chinese Theater and the rest of that tourist-oriented strip of H-wood Boulevard), to Universal City, and, finally, into the depths of the Valley, which you may never need to venture to. The system, which runs as late as midnight, is clean, cool, and usually quite spacious, in part because it's often quite desolate; and since the suits at city hall have finally come around to seeing the benefit of municipal transportation, if you're lucky you'll occasionally be privy to the artist installations (impromptu poetry readings and the like) the MTA has begun to commission at its stations.

As well, the Blue Line (that is an aboveground train system) will take you to Watts and Compton among others and finally to Long Beach in Orange County; while the Green Line, which connects to the Blue, will get you to LAX in those times when you have no upstanding friends—with L.A. traffic, it happens quite often—to take you there. But provided you leave at the right time (or early enough), you're probably better off using a car for such trips. Still, it's good to know that these are here, for no doubt at some point, fed up with the traffic, you'll be tempted to pull your car to the side of the road and leave it there in disgust.

The True L.A. Music Scene

The lead singer of one local, steadfast, unsigned band once told me about the dilemma of the music scene here, and I paraphrase: "Shit, people would f***ing rather go see some stupid f***ing band from Olympia, Washington, than go to one of our damn shows."

Or something along those lines.

Sure, while L.A. has the distinct right to call itself a corporate rock mecca where bands from all over the world come to lose their shirts—and their souls, one might add—and get bad record deals with the Big Five, our resulting curse has been that we, as a gig-going audience, have become a spoiled rotten lot. To our discredit, we've let our own local rock heroes tatter and fray on their poles as we're—more often than not—off at some stupid big-name gig at the House of Blues or trying to get backstage at the Limp Bizkit show. Meanwhile, of course, a small group of less trend-conscious folks do their best to pay the proper tribute by forgoing the $8 parking fees on Sunset Boulevard for more intimate digs where long-established but underappreciated groups like Thelonious Monster and Texas Terri play. While you're here, we (and here is where the paraphrasing ends) f***ing hope you, betwixt your jaunt to Staples Center for the Madonna show, try to do a little of the same. Below are some of our favorite long-lived, small-time, good-rocking bands.

Streetwalkin' Cheetahs—Scary Punk Stuff

I watched in amazement from the balcony of Henry Ford Theater during 2000's *LA Weekly* Music Awards show as Frank Meyer—lead singer and guitarist for the Streetwalkin' Cheetahs— broke a beer bottle, spraying shards of glass on a front-row group consisting of some shocked old-timers slated to accept lifetime achievement awards. Unapologetically, Meyer bellowed, "Rock and roll ain't pretty" into his mic, and the band went on to finish their garagey and galvanizing set. After that, the Cheetahs backed former MC5 guitarist and Los Angeles transplant Wayne Kramer, who did this awesomely massive tune about America's obsession with bombs (the kind we throw in football, and the atomic kind). Later I was told that Meyer also spit at the audience and that he broke one of the event photographer's cameras after the show. From what I hear about the Cheetahs' other gigs, this is nothin'. Formed in L.A. in 1995, this punk quartet, named after a lyric on the Stooges' seminal *Raw Power*, are a hard city fixture that you can easily bang your head and body to—though do be careful of flying debris, please.

Wiskey Biscuit—A Band of Many Genres

The ostensible bar band at Spaceland, this seven-piece hailing from Orange County, has a style which has been dubbed "stoner rock," "country punk," and "countrified Silver Lake." New on the list, with the advent of their second album, *Zig Zag*, is the self-anointed term "country dub" to describe the Biscuit. But *hay*-ell, we just call it good shit. Singer Jason Mason, a spindly, whiny Bob Dylan type with leather wristbands, has the genius stage presence of the ever-pacing Lenny Bruce, or a drunken bum, and the percussionist, he fits in nicely by looking as though he can barely stand half the time. Certainly well underappreciated for having bopped around this town for over a decade (and apparently accepted by other local bands after being dropped by Geffen during the 1995 buyout), these guys are the best thing since sliced pot brownies, Southern style.

The Hangmen—Come for the Headliners, Stay for the Soul

After seeing Concrete Blonde one Sunday night at a local rock club, I figured it was time to get home. But by the time I had said my good-byes and was on my way out the door, the Hangmen had begun their set. I didn't make it past the foyer before I was drawn back by the beautiful, feedback-ridden noise. This L.A. four-piece simply *rocks*. I take that back: They *fucking* rock, which may have something to do with lead singer Bryan Small's tragically clichéd rock past. In a recently released DVD, *Badsville*, which documents the local scene, Small said this after admitting his band had been dropped twice from major labels: "Exactly what goes on in all those *Behind the Music*s is what happened to me, without the limos and, you know, the big money to back it up." Apparently now clean and sober (per the viewing of *Badsville*), Small, along with his Hangmen, hasn't lost his hard edge on the path back from hell. It's good, dirty stuff, like the Stones or the Stooges, the way you should like it.

Texas Terri and the Stiff Ones—Enjoy, But Don't Get Too Close

Texas Terri, another L.A. mainstay, has more rock-and-roll balls than most men. On the night I saw her, we had popped into a dead Zen Café in Silver Lake for last call, and I—hearing a strange cacophony coming from upstairs—felt compelled to investigate.

I'm glad I did; for, in that small concert space, there was Terri and her Stiff Ones playing a maddeningly loud and brash set for a couple of friends. (I later found out someone was having a birthday.) Terri, a well-tattooed rock freak whose high energy and sexually charged frontwoman style is not unlike that of a female Iggy Pop (she, of course, has boobs, which you very well might end up seeing), has been playing round these parts for a good fifteen years–plus now (ever since she moved here from Texas as Terri Laird)—and this is one show you don't want to miss. Meekminded folk might do best to take their seats in the back, however, lest they be bumped into or called on to yell into Terri's own mic; and anyone wearing suede should probably watch out for splashing liquids, which Terri is apt to pour all over herself or—hell, why not?—*you*.

> **Other musical acts to see while visiting Los Angeles:**
> Wayne Kramer (playing with anyone)
> Harry Dean Stanton
> Thelonious Monster (Bob Forrest)
> The Bicycle Thief
> Tsar
> Aimee Mann and/or Michael Penn
> Beachwood Sparks
> Biblical Proof of UFOs
> Silver

Happy-Hour L.A.

One joke about L.A. goes that no one works here. So why would we have such a nice selection of happy hours—that oh-so-fun and cheap way to get drunk and full after a long day at the grind? Because, if you don't count all the out-of-work actors or striking writers in this city, this joke about L.A. is . . . simply that. Here are a couple of our favorite places to go for a fine old happy hour. So a *Resident Tourist* walks into a bar . . .

Steak with a 'Tude

McCormick and Schmick's, a yuppie-level (featuring wood-grain and brass fixtures aplenty) U.S. chain seafood-and-steak number, slums delectably on weekdays (Monday–Thursday 4–7 P.M.; Friday 3–11 P.M.) as a whole mini-menu of stuff takes a dive in price. For $1.95, you can get a plateful of fried calamari or bruschetta topped with shrimp; even a hamburger and fries. The burgers are admittedly a little dry, but hey, did we mention the price? Throw some ketchup on it and be thankful, for once, ya bum! M&S has three L.A.-area locations, but might we suggest, sir (sorry about the bum thing), the Downtown one? Located on the fourth floor of the First Interstate Tower Building, it offers free shuttle service to the Staples Center, the Ahmanson Center, and other area events centers.

McCormick and Schmick's
633 W. Fifth Street at Grand Avenue, Los Angeles
(213) 629-1929

What Nuevo Latino Is, It's Good!

I still don't quite get what Latin fusion is (it may have something to do with liberally mixing the cuisine from various countries where they speak Romance languages, stacking it precariously on ruffly wafers, and serving it all up on pastel plates), but I'm not complaining. From 3 to 7 P.M. on weekdays, this avant-garde (think bold earthy tones and sharp lines intermingling with wavy ones) downtown eatery, owned by the chef team that brought us Border Grill, has a smashing couple of happy hours. At the long bar, suits mingle with trendy in-the-knows, munching on free *cuchifritos* (translated, means "little fried things") and sipping on white sangrias, caparinhas, or—for the less refined—Mexican beers. The suits usually then go on to the heftily priced (this, too, might be a prerequisite for these modern fusion deals) dinners, while the others satisfy themselves on the low-priced appetizers, which include crab cakes and really great cumin fries.

Ciudad
445 S. Figueroa Street, Los Angeles
(213) 486-5171

Two, Two, Two Happy Hours In One Location
Nestled in the back of a Little Tokyo parking lot, this tiny red-bricked building is barely noticeable with all the Japanese lettering and warm, glowing storefronts in the area, but—whooee— it's worth a good couple of clueless drives around the block, that's sure: the darned place, looking on the inside like a cross between an East Coast college pub and the grand *Cheers* TV show bar itself, has two—count them—happy hours, which, in the end, add up to more like a felicitous half-day. The first one (3–7 P.M.) is ostensibly for the after-work crowd, while the other (10 P.M.– close) tends to cater to students of, say, USC (and, sure, those ones of life) willing to brave the stark streets for a little late-night fun, food, and cheap beer. Both of these happy hours feature appetizers at half price and $2 beers, and in both categories the selection is pretty great; as well, the word on the street is that the service is always impeccable. But service schmervice, we say: just get us some of those fries, crab cakes, and a burger with a couple of dozen pitchers to wash it down and you'll be fine.

Weiland's Restaurant and Brewery
400 E. First Street, Downtown
(213) 680-2881

Late-Night L.A.

If the L.A. natives get restless around nine o'clock on a Friday night, they get nervously anxious, apprehensive, and even mad around 1:30 A.M.; closing time, after all, is only a half hour away. The single folks, especially, who've drunk a bunch of funky mixed drinks (and bought some for others, too) in the hopes they would somehow slurringly find their true loves through the sultry barroom haze on this one night of only two in a week that they can really let loose, really feel that crunch even after midnight. For unlike New Orleans or New York, where drunks can continue reeling and saying stupid things to prospective mates all night, apparently L.A. was founded by a bunch of puritans; which means at 2 A.M. the bars close and liquor is no longer sold—no ifs, ands, or buts. Yes, near that point devoted partiers either begin to make expedient attempts to round everybody up to make a sprinting dash to the 7-Eleven drink line or try to hurriedly find an alternate place (preferably with a hot tub) to re-adjourn. At the least, they start getting that nervous tic as they attempt to figure out just exactly how they'll go about making future plans with the pretty stranger sitting across from them. It can all be a real downer. Luckily, all hope is not lost. A couple of our favorite places to go after our unduly harsh early last call follow. . . . Sorry, no alcohol.

Harashimasu mean . . .

No pickup joint, this. (Who in their right mind—besides you, of course—is going to needlessly venture downtown at night?) Koraku is a fun little Japanese version of a late-night diner. (No Denny's, this, either.) Located on the edge of Little Tokyo, and open until 3 A.M. nightly, it's a perfect place for a bunch of buzzed pals to go and soak up some of that straight grain liquor with gyoza, noodles, and rice dishes, and talk about the triumphs of the evening. Good stuff it is, to be sure. Of course, one will easily note through blurry eyes that the clientele tends to be Asian, but then, polite-enough gaijin (the Japanese word for foreigners) are just as accepted; they, too, will hear the word "Harashimasu"— meaning "Welcome"—as they swing open the doors after taking a gander at some of the options in the little glass case out front.

Koraku
314 E. Second Street, Los Angeles
(213) 687-4972

Coffee, Jazz, Pool Tables, Panini—What Else You Need
An arm's length from all the hippest Cahuenga Boulevard
bars, this classy (notice all the brass coffeemakin' fixin's) elixir
shop serves up their caffeine drinks real strong. And God-darned
panini (that's Italian cooked subs) to boot. Plus, the dark lights
keep one from being able to see your ugly mug too well. In the
back, a tattered (be warned, it leans to the right) pool table awaits,
along with a great jukebox and your most favorite retro
videogame tables—those being Ms. Pac Man and Galaga. Collectors will enjoy the for-sale art on the wall and music snobs will
appreciate the occasional jazz act or local folkster who marches
through this place. The hotel only stays open until 3 A.M.; however, after you get enough synthetic energy down your gullet,
you're certain to be ready for whatever late-night debaucherous
experience your friends have in store, those evil sons of guns.
Hotel Café
1623 Cahuenga Boulevard, Los Angeles
(323) 461-2040

Be a Minority, Just Like the Blue Guy
You WASPy types may sometimes feel like the minority at this
24-hour Korean eatery, which tends to bring in mostly Asian
folks. But that's a good thing, especially considering that for just
about forever they've been claiming that in no time at all you'll be
the outnumbered in southern California anyhow.
Of course, people of all races, creeds, and colors are welcome
to try Tofu House's wonderful food and fun atmosphere (note the
pretty garden vista scene on one of the restaurant's walls). And as
if to accentuate this point, the last time my three white-bred bud-
dies and I showed up here after the bars closed, there in the cor-

ner was a young man, dressed all in silver latex, painted blue and donning a cape, enjoying one or another of the house's specialtes: *soon dubu,* a Korean dish of tofu-infused broth with meat, fish, or vegetables that boils so briskly that the raw egg you're given cooks immediately when you crack it into its bowl. We, of course, loved both the *dubu* of the fish variety and some barbecue beef, which, with all the sides that came with these (kimchi; hot, hot crab legs), was enough to feed a whole army of blue dudes (note: it may be rude, but we still suggest ordering one less meal than the number of people in your party); and afterward we did the customary thing by gulping down the soup made when the waiter poured hot water into the remains of our rice bowls. Then we paid our bill and sat outside in the warm evening air enjoying our complimentary melon-flavored gum until a couple of Asian girls said it like they saw it, by calling us annoying white guys. Some things will never change, we guessed, rubbing our satiated bellies and getting in the car . . .

Tofu House
3575 Wilshire Boulevard, Los Angeles
213-382-6677

Index

Vine (bar), 17–18
Vine Boulevard, 37
Vine DMV, 37
Vine Theater, 198
vintage clothing, 138–39,
    152–53, 161–62
Viper Room, xii, 39
Virgil's Hardware, 168–69
Viva Fresh, 73, 75–76
Vroman, A. C., 35
Vroman's Bookstore, 35–36

walking tours, 110
Walk of Fame, 121
Washington Boulevard, Venice,
    136–37
Watts, 115–20
Watts Senior Center Rose
    Garden, 119
Watts Towers, 117–18
waxing studio, 178
Wax Museum, xii, 121
Weiland's Restaurant and
    Brewery, 207
Wendy's California Trail, 13
West Hollywood, 189–90
West Hollywood Park, 71–72
Westminster Senior Citizens
    Center, 65
Westside Rentals, 149–50
Westwood Recreation
    Complex, 57

whale watching, 70
The Whisky à Go-Go, 20,
    29–30, 39
White, Emil, 48
The White Horse, 15–16
Willis, Jim, 115
Wilshire Boulevard, 134
wine, 168
wineries, 94–95
winos, 135–36
Wiskey Biscuit, 203–4
The World Café at The Ruby,
    95–96
World Modeling Agency, 6
World on Wheels, 195–96
Wound & Wound Toy Co., 132,
    169–70
www.seeing-stars.com, 192–93
Wyman, George, 106

X-rated movies, 1–7

yard sales, 170
The Yellow Balloon, 178–79
Ye Rustic Café, 97
YMCA, 57
yoga, 55
Y-QUE, 141–42

zoos, 50, 65
    petting, 173
Zzxyx sign, 49